SHEET MUSIC

Sheet Music

Uncovering the Secrets of Sexual Intimacy in Marriage

DR. KEVIN LEMAN

Tyndale House Publishers, Inc.
Carol Stream, Illinois

Visit Tyndale's exciting Web site at www.tyndale.com

TYNDALE and Tyndale's quill logo are registered trademarks of Tyndale House Publishers, Inc.

Sheet Music

Edited by Ramona Cramer Tucker

Library of Congress Cataloging-in-Publication Data

Leman, Kevin.
  Sheet music : uncovering the secrets of sexual intimacy in marriage / Kevin Leman.
    p. cm.
Includes bibliographical references.
ISBN-13: 978-0-8423-6023-4
ISBN-10: 0-8423-6023-9
ISBN-13: 978-0-8423-6024-1 (pbk.)
ISBN-10: 0-8423-6024-7 (pbk.)
1. Sex in marriage. 2. Sex instruction. 3. Sex. 4. Intimacy (Psychology). I. Title.
HQ734 .L386 2003
613.9'6—dc21   2002011943

Printed in the United States of America

10 09 08 07 06
12 11 10 9 8

To my son-in-law, Dennis O'Reilly,
and his lovely bride, my daughter Krissy.

Go ahead and create a symphony!
And maybe a few kids as well. . . .

Contents

NOTE *to the* READER

Some of what you'll read in this book may be too blunt or straightforward for your personal taste. Every person's view on sex (and his or her background, which informs thought and relational patterns) differs. However, if you're willing to forge ahead for the sake of the best marriage you can imagine, then this book is for you. It will expand and challenge your thinking about sex. Instead of just a how-to-do-it manual, it's more of a do-it-yourself look at why to do it and how to do it better.

Sheet Music: Uncovering the Secrets of Sexual Intimacy in Marriage isn't intended to make you feel guilty for what you have or haven't done, but rather to help you pinpoint what goes on in your brain and in your relationship with your spouse (or spouse-to-be) so you can have an active, fulfilling sex life.

If you're currently in premarital counseling, read chapters 1 through 4 and the "For Men Only" and "For Women Only" chapters. But please stop there—and wait to read the rest until after you're married.

A Tale of Two Couples

Jim and Karen were both virgins when they got married twenty-one years ago. Like many young couples, they had fairly unrealistic views of what sex would be like. "Hit and miss" might be a pretty good description of their sex life after the honeymoon; they never really got a handle on things until almost fifteen years into their marriage.

Here's what happened. Jim was always looking for (and worse, thinking he had found) the "magic bullet." He tried something new—the way he held Karen, cradled her, or tenderly touched a delicate spot—and he tuned in to her moans, thinking, *Okay, this is the key; this will unlock her sexual fury.*

While Karen really did enjoy that new touch, she learned to be conservative with her moans because once Jim heard one, he was certain to do *the exact same thing* for the next fifty to one hundred times they made love. Karen never understood why it took one hundred times of silence to overcome one moan, but that's the way it was with Jim. He became so predictable that what once made her hotter than an August day now turned her into a glacier. Jim would just get frustrated, thinking (but never verbalizing), *I know I'm doing this right. It worked that one time! Why isn't it working now? I must not be doing it soft enough (or fast enough, or some other variation).*

When I first met with Jim, I gave him a simple assignment. "Jim," I said, "I want you to go home, look at your wife's closet, then look at yours. Tell me if you notice anything different."

"I don't have to go home to do that, Dr. Leman," he said. "I know our closets by memory."

"Okay, then. When you look at the shoes, do you notice anything different?"

"Yeah, she has fifty pairs and I have three."

"Let me guess—business shoes, tennis shoes, and work-in-the-yard shoes."

"That's right."

"Now, if you counted her outfits and then counted yours, what would you find?"

"I'd need a calculator for her outfits, but I could count mine using my ten fingers."

"What does that tell you?"

"That she likes to buy clothes?"

"Well, yes, but in regard to sex, what does it mean?"

"Well, she doesn't have many sexy outfits, if that's what you're getting at."

Seeing that subtlety wasn't Jim's strength, I decided to lay it out for him more directly. "Jim, what I'm trying to say is that your wife appears to like a little more variety than you do. She doesn't want to wear the same dress on Monday, Wednesday, and Friday. In fact, she may not want to wear the same outfit every other Monday. She wants variety.

"You see, some of us guys treat sex like a football playbook. We know what we're going to do, how we're going to do it, and where we're going to end up. The problem with this is that our wives soon grow bored with the routine. They could chart our movements and predict, within about ten seconds, how long we're going to spend upstairs before we go downstairs. Your wife wants more than that."

I saw a lightbulb go on in Jim's mind. What I was saying was making sense.

"Here's your job, Jim," I continued. "Your wife will not be the same woman on Tuesday evening, sexually, that she was on Saturday morning. One night she may be up for adventure or a rushed quickie. She'll want you just to 'take her.' Some mornings she may want slow, languid sex, with you taking a lot of time to convince her that she's up for it. Your job is to figure out which way the wind is blowing on that particular day."

It didn't take much more than that. I didn't need to send Jim to a "sex surrogate" (nor would I ever do such a thing). He didn't have to watch some videos. He didn't need to buy a hundred dollars worth of "marital aids." In fact, Jim realized, as I wrote in another book, that sex begins in the kitchen—it's an all-day affair. He adopted a new mind-set and, according to Karen, became a virtuoso of the bedroom.

Now, seven years later, sex permeates virtually everything Jim and Karen do. If you haven't experienced this, you wouldn't believe what an amazing marital "glue" good sex can be. Three years ago, Jim was trapped in a job that he hated. His boss was determined to become the most hated man east of the Mississippi. When you're in your mid-forties, feeling trapped is about the worst feeling there is. Jim could barely force himself to go into the office, but with twins who were in middle school (with college in the not-too-distant future), and two toddlers just getting into grade school, he didn't have a choice. Now was not the time to make a risky financial change.

One Friday Jim got an e-mail from Karen. It was the first thing he saw when he sat down in his office:

```
Great news! The younger kids are going to
be at Grandma's house tonight and the
older boys will be gone at youth group. I
made reservations for eight at Palazzi's
[Jim's favorite restaurant]. If you can come home
by six, that'll give us a good hour and a
half to enjoy the hors d'oeuvres—which I
plan to be "wearing." By the way, if you
look in your briefcase, you'll find a
Polaroid. Consider it your predinner
"menu." Can't wait to see you.
Your Karen
```

You know what Jim said to himself after reading that e-mail? Keep in mind, he was in a dead-end job; financial pressures were mounting. His boss was a jerk who made Jim's daily existence a living hell. But even so, Jim closed the e-mail and said to himself, "I'm the luckiest man alive."

Having a great sex life is an exhilarating experience; it can bond a husband and wife in a way that's unequaled in human experience. Knowing that your bride really does care for you, that your husband desires your body more than anything else, affirms a man and a woman in profound and multiple ways.

Jim and Karen's kids benefited greatly from this e-mail, by the way. When Jim and Karen finally picked up the younger kids from Grandma's house, Jim couldn't wait to see them. Because he was sexually satisfied, he could focus fully on being there for his kids, hearing about their day, and taking the time to tuck them into bed. And don't think that the kids didn't notice how affectionate Jim and Karen were that evening. It gave them a sense of security and happiness, making *them* think, *We're in the best family anyone could be in.*

Sexual fulfillment didn't come overnight for Jim and Karen. But when it came, it changed everything about their home. To tell you the truth, Jim would die for Karen; he'd take a bullet for her without thinking twice. There's nothing he wouldn't do for her.

~⊙~

Mark and Brenda faced a sexual challenge of their own. They had been sexually active before marriage, and both admit that the sex was pretty exciting. But, predictably for couples who engage in sexual relations before marriage, sexual relations cooled off not that long after the wedding. Mark didn't seem as eager as he had been before, and Brenda was far less adventurous.

At first Mark and Brenda thought it was just the kids. They got pregnant early on in their marriage and now had two kids under the age of five. Over time, however, sex became even less frequent, until eventually it was almost an embarrassing afterthought, something the two of them did because they thought, well, they should—at least once a month, anyway.

Mark had a well-paying job and a good boss, but he was under tremendous stress. As a salesman, if Mark performed well, he was rewarded handsomely. If he fell into the bottom third, he'd be fired. He was only as good as last quarter's numbers.

Mark thought he had an account worth several hundred thousand dollars in the bag; it was just a matter of getting the company to sign. When he went into the purchaser's office, however, he was shocked to hear, "I'm sorry, Mark, but we've decided to go with someone else."

"You've got to be kidding! We've been working on this for two months, and last week you said it looked like a go. What do we need to do to earn back your business?"

"It's too late for that," the purchaser replied. "We've already signed another contract."

Stunned, Mark walked out to his car in a daze. He instinctively answered his cell phone when it rang but immediately wished he hadn't.

"Hey, Mark!" his boss yelled through the phone. "I thought I'd take you out to that new Italian restaurant for lunch to celebrate your closing of that Andreeson account."

Mark wanted to swallow the cell phone right there.

Five hours later, after a lonely and very alcohol-laden lunch, Mark began to reflect on what his life had become. He had earned a six-figure income last year, but his job security was always on the line—as his boss reminded him when he heard the news about the Andreeson account.

How long had it been since he and Brenda had had any fun? Mark remembered the days they couldn't keep their hands off each other; now they were like two roommates sharing the same bed but not much else. Ever since the kids arrived, they seemed boxed into that (admittedly gorgeous) 3,500-square-foot home. Mark yearned for the days when he and Brenda could make the world disappear for a few hours as they got lost in each other's embrace.

Deciding to make a change, Mark called Brenda and confessed, "I've had a really crummy day. Can we just go out tonight?"

It was an emotional cry from Mark—even more than a physical one—but Brenda didn't understand. She'd had a rushed day herself. And because she'd lost touch with her husband and wasn't able to read the emotion in his request, she responded with a curt, "Mark, it's five o'clock! I can't get a babysitter this late. What are you thinking? You *never* give me any notice."

Mark wanted to tell Brenda that he missed her. He longed for her to be the eager woman she used to be, who was willing to cut classes to "fool around" for a little bit. But he had already stuck out his neck once today, and look where that got him! So he went on the defensive.

"Ah, forget it," he said, and hung up the phone.

Mark stopped at a pub on the way home and shot pool until

11 P.M. He knew he'd catch a lot of flak from Brenda for being out so late, but she didn't understand the pressure he was under.

Brenda also didn't understand that Mark masturbated two or three times a week—and every time he did so, he felt his desire for Brenda as a person decline just a little bit more. He was tired of being reluctantly accommodated and never pursued.

For her part, Brenda was too busy with the kids to notice. In fact, she was actually thankful that Mark didn't pressure her for sex anymore; she was too tired to even think about it. It never occurred to her that Mark was taking matters "into his own hands" and was adept enough at hiding the pornography on the computer that she never found it.

What Brenda didn't realize was how much this sexual winter was costing them as a couple, and how, if they didn't turn things around, they'd probably be divorced within another five years.

The kids noticed that Mommy and Daddy were rarely affectionate toward each other and often very impatient. They could sense there was something "under the surface," a seething discontent. But because it was never brought out into the open, they lived with the fear and lack of security that such an environment creates.

Brenda became more and more focused on her kids, trying to meet her emotional emptiness through her children's affection. Mark became more interested in work and his computer at home.

Both lived out the sad truth depicted in this anonymous poem.

The Wall

Their wedding picture mocked them from the table,
These two whose minds no longer touched each other.

They lived with such a heavy barricade between them
That neither battering ram of words
Nor artilleries of touch could break it down.

Somewhere, between the oldest child's first tooth
And the youngest daughter's graduation,
They lost each other.

Throughout the years each slowly unraveled
That tangled ball of string called self,
And as they tugged at stubborn knots,
Each hid his searching from the other.

Sometimes she cried at night
And begged the whispering darkness to tell her who she was.

He lay beside her, snoring like a hibernating bear,
Unaware of her winter.

Once, after they had made love,
He wanted to tell her how afraid he was of dying,
But, fearing to show his naked soul,
He spoke instead about the beauty of her breasts.

She took a course in modern art,
Trying to find herself in colors splashed upon a canvas,
Complaining to other women about men who are insensitive.

He climbed into a tomb called "The Office,"
Wrapped his mind in a shroud of paper figures,
And buried himself in customers.

Slowly, the wall between them rose,
Cemented by the mortar of indifference.

One day, reaching out to touch each other
They found a barrier they could not penetrate,
And recoiling from the coldness of the stone,
Each retreated from the stranger on the other side.

For when love dies, it is not in a moment of angry battle,
Nor when fiery bodies lose their heat.

It lies panting, exhausted,
Expiring at the bottom of a wall it could not scale.

⁓◈⁓

Two couples. Two stories. One reality. If you think sex isn't important, you are sadly mistaken. Many people have been wounded by sex and hurt by sexual memories. (We'll talk about this in a later chapter.) But if you're married, sex will be one of the most important parts of your life, whether you want it to be that way or not. If you don't treat sex this way—as a matter of supreme importance—you're shortchanging yourself, your spouse, and your kids.

This might, in fact, be a hard book to read. It certainly was a hard book to write, because in our society today we have a difficult time talking about sex. Oh, we *joke* about sex, degrading it through filthy stories, movies, and magazines, but we never talk about marital sex in the way the Creator designed it. Marital sex—the most important and only appropriate kind, in my view—gets ignored, and couples pay a fearful price when this sad reality happens.

But when you give people permission to talk about sex in a nonthreatening environment, you can't shut them up! Once they get going, they want to talk about sex because they know that sex is a powerful force in our married lives.

My hope is that this book will expand and challenge your thinking about sex. It's not just a how-to-do-it manual; the physical mechanics aren't that difficult. This is more of a do-it-yourself look at why to do it and how to do it better. I want to reawaken in you the shared experience of enjoying this wonderful gift on your journey with your mate. This is not a book that should make you feel guilty, but rather it should expand your thinking and the possibility that you too can have an active, fulfilling sex life with the one you love.

This book may not have all the answers, but it does have a

lot of them. I'm not a sexual therapist; I'm a psychologist. While we'll talk about the physical side of sex, my specialty is with what goes on in your brain and in your relationship. That's where most marriages need to be healed first.

Besides, the physical aspect will usually take care of itself if the relationship is healthy. If you decide to become sexually adventurous as a couple, you're not going to do things perfectly, anyway; you're going to fail, and hopefully, you'll laugh about it when you do. Nobody's sex life is such that every experience is a ten. You may have to be satisfied with regular eights or sixes and even an occasional three.

But this book is written for you, as a couple, to help you understand what a unique and wonderful gift you are to each other, as well as the unique and wonderful ways you can express your love in a very physical and pleasurable sense.

From my experience of working with thousands of couples, I've become convinced that this wonderful gift of sex makes everything nicer. A couple's sex life is usually a microcosm of the marriage. Every now and then a couple has a great sex life with a poor marriage, but this is the rarity, something you see only every couple of years. Most often, if the marriage is on the rocks, sex will follow it to the bottom.

OUR DEEPEST DESIRES

I want to say a word to the men right at the start of this book. I know, I know—you can't wait until we start getting to the really good parts. But first let me put marital sex into a completely different context. You need to know that every day a woman internally asks her husband, *Do you really love me? Do you really care?*

How does she measure that love? How does she know she's truly cared for? It's usually not in the bedroom. If anything turns off a woman, it's the feeling that all her husband cares about is sex. If a wife thinks her main role is to be a willing recipient of her husband's sexual advances, she feels demeaned and disrespected.

Men, if your attitude has become, *Well, honey, are you gonna put out tonight or not?* you don't realize how much you're missing. With that attitude all you're going to get—at best—is an accommodating wife, but never an eager one. I can give you the best sexual technique in the world, but with that attitude, your sexual life is still going to wind up in the pits.

What warms a woman up is when her husband helps around the house, picks up after himself, helps with the children, makes arrangements for dates, and overall *cares for her.* If a husband consistently and graciously does this without acting like a martyr, he's going to find, six times out of ten, that his wife is ready and eager to enjoy an active and fulfilling love life. It will be a natural response to a lifestyle of sincere affection.

Let's talk about the six in ten. Women, this might surprise you, but even more than your husband wants to have sex with you for his own sexual relief, the truth is, he wants to please you even more than he wants to be pleasured. It might seem like it's all about him, but what he really wants, emotionally, is to see how much you enjoy the pleasure he can give you. If he fails to do that, for any reason, he'll end up feeling inadequate, lonely, and unloved. Most of us men want to be our wives' heroes.

It's my theory that the little boys we men once were, we still are. We still want to please the primary woman in our life. When we were six, that meant pleasing Mommy; when we're twenty-six (or thirty-six, or forty-six, or sixty-six), it's our bride.

When sex dies in a marriage, a man loses something very important to him—the knowledge that he can please his wife physically. And a woman loses the satisfaction that she has a man who is enthralled with her beauty.

Because sex is so intimate to who we are as men and women, it becomes intricately tied up with the smallest element of every marriage. If a couple spent just ten minutes describing their sex life to me, I'd have a pretty good handle on what's happening in the rest of their marriage. So while I want to help you improve your sexual technique, I also want to remind you that sex is part of a *relationship*.

GOURMET SEX

Just about anybody can "biologically" perform the act of sexual intercourse, just as any five-year-old can make a peanut-butter sandwich. But if you want a gourmet meal, you need to find a chef.

For example, anybody can cook a fish. You can take the slippery sucker out of the water, not bother to gut it or descale it but just throw it in a pan without any spices or preparation, and it'll cook. You'll be able to bite through those scales, pick the innards out of your teeth, but still get some healthy fish to swallow. You've cooked a fish.

But it's going to taste fishy if you do it that way, and good fish does not taste fishy. I know what I'm talking about here. My Swedish-Norwegian uncles were fisherman. Man, did they know how to prepare a fish!

I remember one time as a young kid, my uncle asked me, "Do you like to eat fish, boy?"

"No."

"You'd like this fish."

"No, thank you," I said in my squeaky boy's voice. "I don't eat fish. I don't like fish."

He smiled a knowing smile, then took out a nice shiny quarter. "Would you try just one bite if I gave you this?"

Back in those days, a quarter could get you a whole lot more than a gumball, so I took the offer. But I didn't stop at one bite; I ate thirteen of those little suckers. I'd never tasted anything so good in my entire life!

The difference is, my uncle knew what he was doing. He

carefully filleted the fish, expertly removing all the bones. Then he put the fish in saltwater, which draws out the blood and other things you don't want in there. Then he dipped the fish in pancake batter and fried it up just right.

A chef isn't a "born" cook. He goes to school, studies the art of cooking, masters the use of herbs and flavors and presentation, and then experiments with what works best. A good sexual "chef" does the same thing. A loving husband will soon learn that presentation means everything to a woman. To truly engage a wife's senses, a husband needs to be aware of how he presents himself for sex. Because men have hair triggers, presentation often gets ignored, and the man is clumsy, awkward, or even offensive in the way he approaches his wife for sexual intimacy.

Trust me, men: How you present your "hunk of burning love" really matters, and it's something that needs to be put in context. Your wife wants to know you're a good father, as well as a kind and generous person, every bit as much as she wants to know you can touch all the right places.

Too many married couples settle for second best. The husband is willing to use his wife for biological release, and the wife may be willing to "accommodate" her husband just to avoid his incessant nagging (and, sometimes, outright begging). But that's not what either of them truly desires. Neither person is fulfilled when sex is desperately asked for and only grudgingly given.

So take the plunge! Joyfully move from "peanut butter and jelly sex" to gourmet intimacy. Don't settle for less than God has intended. Sex is one of the most amazing things God ever thought up—but sex this good doesn't come naturally to any one of us. We have to become willing to practice how to be a better lover; we need to spend time thinking of ways to keep sex fresh and fun; we even need to study our spouse to discover just what fulfills them sexually.

Some of you might be asking, "But Doc, is it worth the effort?" Is it worth the effort?! If you could see into the future and experience just a taste of what a fulfilling sex life can do for your marriage, my guess is that you'd be willing to invest a whole lot more time than you're investing now. You'd be begging me to tell you more.

In addition to gourmet sex, there's what I like to call "designer" sex.

DESIGNER SEX

"Do all men think about sex all the time?" a woman asked me in obvious exasperation after I'd talked about the differences between men and women.

"Well, not *all* the time," I said, noting the relief cover her face until I added, "sometimes we think about food *and* sex. Occasionally we think about killing deer and breaking ninety on the golf course, but pretty much our minds go back to sex."

"Aren't there any men who are holy and have pure minds?" she went on.

See, that's the problem right there: She's assuming that when I say most men think about sex a large percentage of the time, I mean we're thinking *dirty* thoughts. Some people of faith think God and sex have about as much in common as football and ice dancing. Just because a man thinks about sex a lot doesn't mean he's thinking impure thoughts. If he's imagining what another woman (besides his wife) looks like naked, or how good she'd be in bed, then yes, he's polluting his mind. But if he's imagining how good it would feel to rub massage oil all over his wife later that night while on his way to giving her a body-to-body massage, he's being as pure as an inner-city mission worker serving a bowl of soup to the homeless.

Who is the giver of all good gifts? God. Sex is a gift from God and a commandment from God. When God tells us to be "fruitful and multiply," he's not talking about apples and cloning. He's talking about having sexual intercourse and giving birth to babies.

Author Stephen Schwambach writes:

> Anybody who has ever experienced great lovemaking instinctively knows the truth: Sex is too good to have just happened. It didn't evolve as the result of some cosmic accident. Something this exquisite had to have been lovingly, brilliantly, creatively designed.
>
> If an atheist ever comes up to you and demands proof that there is a God, all you have to answer is one word: "Sex." Give him a day to think about it. If at the end of that day he remains unconvinced, then he has just revealed far more about his sex life—or the lack thereof—than he ever intended!
>
> God created sex. Doesn't that tell you a lot about who God really is? Among other things, it tells you that He is ingenious.[1]

"Designer sex" is sex as the Creator intended it; sex that uses his manual as a guide. Observant Jews and Christians both believe that sex as God designed it is sex only within marriage.

Why do you think God reserves sex for marriage? I believe that one of the reasons (which gets very little attention, unfortunately) is that good sex is not easy and it's very personal. Think about it: A man is given the daunting task of trying to read how to set his bride's sails in changing winds. Sometimes she wants to run free and loose; other times she wants to tack back and forth, keeping things in check. If the husband is going to be the captain of her heart, he has to learn how to read the winds, and that takes a lot of time and a lot of experience

[1]Stephen and Judith Schwambach, *For Lovers Only* (Eugene, Ore: Harvest House, 1990), 127.

with the same woman. Experience with other women will lead him astray more than help him, because every woman is unique in her desire and pleasure.

Think about it this way: If you've had sex with nine women, put nine watches on your arm—five on one arm and four on the other. Now let me ask you, what time is it? It becomes so complicated trying to average the nine watches that you're much better off having just one watch, even if that timepiece is off by a couple minutes.

In the same way, the wife is also charged with understanding her husband so well that she intuitively knows when her husband needs her to initiate sex or when he needs her to allow herself to be vanquished in a holy and profound way. She should actually study her husband's spoken and unspoken sexual needs and desires as vigorously as she did any textbook before a major test in high school or college. After all, this isn't just an academic exercise. This is her marriage!

Designer sex is about more than familiarity, however. It's also about respect. I've heard a lot of women say some very hurtful and disrespectful things about men in general and their husbands in particular: "He's always ready for sex with whomever or whatever." "He thinks through his fly." A woman minimizes a man when she says that all he cares about is sex; she betrays her ignorance about the complexity of a man's soul and the interconnectedness of our spirituality and physical being. What she doesn't realize is that sex represents many different things to a man. A number of them are emotional and spiritual, having nothing to do with the physical. I'm your average Joe who doesn't have eight buddies to talk about life with, like most women do. All I've got is my wife, and if she's too busy with the kids and I repeatedly get sent into the dugout, I tell myself, *She doesn't care. She doesn't know what I'm up against.*

Sometimes we men do act like little boys. I'm not saying

that's good or admirable, but that's the way we are. You're married to a real man, not an ideal stoic—and if he is denied sexual fulfillment, it will affect him in more ways than a woman could possibly understand.

One of the most loving and holy things you can do in marriage is to provide a sexually fulfilling pursuit of your husband or wife. Therefore, without apology, this is going to be the most explicit book I've ever written (which is why, I have to confess, it has been harder to write than any other). I want to teach you how to be an extravagant lover. I want your spouse to go to sleep with a smile on his or her face thinking, *I've got to be the happiest guy/girl in the world!*

But before you read on, let me give you a few warnings.

WARNING!

I'm not ashamed to say that sex is one of my favorite subjects. There is little I don't like about sex between a married husband and wife. Whenever someone asks me, "Dr. Leman, what's the best position for sex?" I always respond, "*Any* position is good if it gets the job done!"

Notice I didn't say that any *sexual experience* is good, because I believe that any sexual experience outside of marriage is ultimately destructive. If you are not married (or not going through premarital counseling—more on this in a moment), then this book is not for you. The advice I'm giving about exploring creativity in sexuality is meant for committed couples, not for those who are living together or sleeping together outside of marriage.

If you are having sex before marriage, you are ultimately threatening your own happiness and marital satisfaction. The research couldn't be clearer:

1. A national study of over 1,800 married couples indicated that the probability of getting a divorce was twice as high

for couples who had cohabited prior to marriage compared to those couples who had not. In addition, cohabitation prior to marriage related to lower levels of subsequent marital interaction and higher levels of marital disagreement and instability.[2]

2. A study of 3,884 Canadian women indicated that women who had cohabited before marriage were 50 percent more likely to get a divorce than women who had not cohabited before marriage. Of the cohabiting women, 35 percent could be expected to divorce within fifteen years of marriage compared to only 19 percent among those who had not cohabited prior to marriage.[3]

3. A study of 4,300 Swedish women ages twenty to forty-four indicated that those who had cohabited before marriage had divorce rates that were 80 percent higher than women who had not cohabited before marriage.[4]

4. A study using a nationally representative sample of 1,235 women ages twenty to thirty-seven indicated that married women who had cohabited prior to marriage were 3.3 times more likely to have sex with someone other than their husband than married women who had not cohabited prior to marriage. Single women who cohabited were 1.7 times more likely to have a secondary sex partner than single women who did not live with their partners.[5]

So then, if you are living with someone outside of marriage, I suggest you move out and start over. The two of you may

[2]Alan Booth and David Johnson, "Premarital Co-habitation and Marital Success," *Journal of Family Issues* 9 (1988): 261–270. This and several other citations in this section are taken from Wade Horn, *Father Facts* (Gaithersburg, Md.: The National Fatherhood Initiative, third edition, no date given), 46ff.
[3]T. R. Balakrishnan et al., "A Hazard Model of the Covariates of Marriage Dissolution in Canada," *Demography* 24 (1987): 395–406.
[4]Neil Bennett, Ann Klimas Blanc, and David E. Bloom, "Commitment and the Modern Union: Assessing the Link Between Cohabitation and Subsequent Marital Instability," *American Sociological Review* 53 (1988): 127–138.
[5]Renata Forste and Koray Tanfer, "Sexual Exclusivity among Dating, Cohabiting, and Married Women," *Journal of Marriage and the Family* 58 (1996): 33–47.

still make it work, but if you can't make it work outside of marriage without being sexually active, odds are that the marriage will soon fall apart anyway.

Now some of you are thinking, *This Dr. Leman guy is nuts—a holdover from the Victorian era!* Not so. Before you close this book and go on with life, let me remind you that today's average marriage lasts just seven years. This is a pathetic shadow of what marriage used to be. Obviously, what we're doing today in our society—sex on the first or second date—isn't working for us. It may help singles cope with sexual frustration in the short run, but it destroys meaningful marriages in the long run.

Maybe we ought to try it a new way.

After unmarried people, the second group I want to warn away from this book consists of those people who are uncomfortable talking about sex in a forthright manner. I have talked about sex in front of some adults who practically attempted to crawl under the floor when I had participants start to list slang words for the male genitalia. (You wouldn't believe how silent it got when I followed up with, "And now, what about the female genitalia?").

I'll be honest with you: Probably everybody will be offended by at least one thing I say in this book. If you don't like one particular point, that's okay. You paid for this book if you didn't get it out of the library, so rip out the page, throw it away, and focus on the rest. It won't bug me—but I owe it to you to be straightforward and provocative.

Some people hear the word *sex* and think, *All right! It's about time. Give it to me straight, Leman, and don't hold back on any of the details!* These folks are like my best friend Moonhead, who likes to remind me, "Leman, it's not good sex if you don't need to take a shower afterwards." They would be offended only if I dabbled in clichés to avoid sounding provocative.

Other people can barely mouth the word *sex* and keep a straight face. I understand this. Few things are more private and more personal than sexual activity between a husband and a wife. These people think it is impossible to even mention the basics of sexual anatomy and activity without getting into bad taste or immorality.

I want to warn you up front: I'm going to be very explicit and frank in this book. If specific descriptions of sexual acts offend you or you find discussions of sexual creativity within marriage to be distasteful, please know that it isn't my intention to cause an offense. The church is filled with many people from many different backgrounds, and we need all of them. However, I encourage you to cherish your spouse enough to risk opening the door to exploring new ways to increase your sexual intimacy. Although some statements in this book may make you uncomfortable, keep reading with an open mind—take the challenge to think creatively about this important aspect of your marriage.

Finally, allow me, as a psychologist, to give a word of warning to premarital couples who will be using this book. I recommend that you save the second half for the honeymoon. You will find it helpful to read the chapters up through the one dealing with your first night together, because that information will serve you well on your honeymoon. You'll also benefit from the chapters entitled "For Men Only" and "For Women Only." But please stop there until after you're married. Reading together explicit descriptions of sexual activities when you cannot morally engage in those activities is a temptation you don't need to bring into your life at this point. Trust me on this one: Couples rarely suffer from a lack of information as much as they suffer from a lack of innocence in the marital bed. You can make up for a lack of information after you're married; the lack of innocence will mark your relationship for life. Give each other the best wedding gift and the best honeymoon available: pure bodies, pure love, and pure intentions. Once you understand the basics you'll have plenty to hold you until after the wedding, at which point you can feast to your heart's delight—with God's blessing and good pleasure! So bring the book along for the honeymoon—but be willing to wait until then.

If you're still reading, welcome aboard! I can't wait to get going.

2

A Crowded Bed

*Y*our marriage bed is one of the most crowded places on the face of the earth. It is teeming with people, some of whom you've never met, but they're all there—all affecting your sexual intimacy, looking over your shoulder, and shaping the quality of your sexual pleasure.

Don't look behind the pillow, but be aware that your parents are lurking right underneath it! And if you think that's bad, you also better get used to your in-laws, who are hiding under your spouse's pillow!

At the foot of the bed? Oh, that's your and your spouse's siblings. Underneath the bed? Don't even get me started on that!

What am I talking about?

You come into marriage with more baggage than you know. This baggage has formed into what I call your "rulebook"—unconscious but very influential beliefs you hold about how things should be done (especially in bed). A big part of my counseling practice is devoted to helping people understand their rulebook, because a person's rulebook governs everything about his or her life, especially sexuality.

"But Dr. Leman," you might say, "I didn't know I had a rulebook!"

Few of us do, but all of us get furious when a rule from our rulebook is broken. A husband will ultimately pay for the mistakes of his father-in-law, just as a wife will pay dearly for the mistakes of her mother-in-law. You're not getting married to a person without a past. You're going to bed with a person who has been indelibly imprinted by his order of birth, her parents' style of child rearing, and his early childhood experiences. She may be naked when she comes to bed, but the last thing she is is alone.

Since I deal extensively with rulebooks in another book, *The New Birth Order Book: Why You Are the Way You Are,* in this book I'm going to limit myself to talking about how rulebooks affect us in bed.

YOUR SEXUAL RULEBOOK

Cheryl wants to be surprised by sex; she wants spontaneity, creativity, and variety. She is most offended by boredom, and she wants her husband to always keep her guessing about what's next. One of Cheryl's favorite sexual memories is when her husband brought home a bottle of baby oil and a tarp to put over the bedsheets. The two spouses slid all over each other and created quite a mess, but it was spontaneous, created a lot of laughs, and Cheryl had the time of her life.

Melissa hates to be shocked. She wants to know what's going to happen at least twenty-four hours ahead of time. If she and her husband are going to be naked at the same time, there must be a towel beneath both of them before either partner exchanges any bodily fluids, lest those same bodily fluids actually touch the sheet. Both partners must be properly showered and all teeth must be brushed within thirty minutes of beginning sex. The thought of making a huge mess or a huge noise would turn her off instead of turn her on. If Melissa's husband brought home a bottle of baby oil, she'd say, "And just what do you think you're going to do with that? It'll take me half a day just to clean up the mess! Have you ever tried to wipe that stuff up?"

Why the difference?

Ted wants his wife to be the sexual aggressor. He loves it when she pushes him over and jumps on top; it's the most thrilling thing he's ever known to watch his wife actively take part in the sexual act and actually work to find the position where she receives the most stimulation. And when she's expressive about how good she's feeling, Ted can barely contain his excitement.

Andy has to be in control at all times; he takes any initiative from his wife as a challenge to his own masculinity. He decides what they do, when they do it, and how they do it, no arguments allowed.

Why are two men so very different?

One of the great pitfalls in writing a book like this is that no two men and no two women are alike. Men can be just as different from other men as genders can be different from each other. While we can make generalizations, every stereotype will be proven false by somebody, which is why individual communication is so crucial in a marriage. I can give you advice about what most men like, but that very advice might really turn your husband off. There really is no substitute for a married couple reading this book together and discussing the chapters as they go along.

What accounts for this great variety in styles of lovemaking? Nine times out of ten, it has to do with a person's rulebook. Cheryl's rulebook says, "Sex is more enjoyable when it's fun and spontaneous; life is too short to do anything the same way twice." Melissa's rulebook says, "Sex needs to be governed by strict standards, lest it get out of hand." Jim's rulebook says, "Sex is most meaningful when my wife pursues me and shows she wants me," while Andy's rulebook says, "Sex is okay only when I'm in charge."

These rulebooks are shaped by our response to our childhood experiences, our upbringing, and our birth order. Rulebooks within families will usually have some similarities, but they will also have marked differences. Ultimately, your rulebook is a very individual thing, and it governs virtually everything you do.

The thing about rulebooks is that they are often unconscious. Melissa probably can't explain why she just *has* to have a towel under her any more than Andy could articulate why he'd go crazy if his wife tried to take control. But these unconscious rules govern every act of sex they've ever been a part of.

Understanding Your Sexual Rulebook

Parental influences

To begin discovering these unwritten and often unconscious rules, ask yourself a few questions:

- What gets me most upset in bed?
- What, in general, most fulfills me sexually?
- What makes me lose all interest in sex?
- What generates the most interest in sex?
- What sexual request or act creates the most fear in me?

Now step back and ask yourself why this might be so. Why does the thought of oral sex disgust me, when so many others find it exciting? Why does having the light on make me feel cold sexually, when it arouses others? Why do I need my spouse to be the one who always initiates sexual intimacy?

Part of the answer might be how you were brought up to think about sex. Some people, particularly from very religious households, were taught that sex is something best never spoken of. "Yes, sex is necessary to populate the world, but let's pretend that it doesn't even exist the rest of the time!" If a person grows up in this environment, he or she may never feel fully free to let go and enjoy the sexual experience for its own sake.

Here's why you want to ask yourself these questions and bring the "hidden influence" out into the open: Once you understand the influence, you can decide whether it's a healthy or unhealthy one. You can choose to keep it or, if it's hindering your marriage, get rid of it.

So ask yourself these questions. Were your parents affectionate? Did you have the kind of mom who always slapped her husband's hands away when he tried to flirt with her? Was your dad uncommonly cold toward you and your mom? Did he use his hand only to hurt and never to caress? Most importantly, has this style of parenting warped your view of sexual expression?

Maybe you had the opposite problem and your parents turned you off by being libertines. Perhaps as a young girl you found some pornography in your dad's bedroom, and the sight of those pictures disgusted you, making you say, "I'm never going to do anything like that." Even worse, you might have been abused, making it all but impossible for you to trust another man. Every touch feels like a violation, even though you know your husband loves you.

Sadly, many husbands don't even know their wives were sexually abused. I can't tell you how many times in my private practice I've been the first one to find out—the first person the abused woman ever shared her misery with. It amazes me that a guy who has been married for ten or even fifteen years doesn't know how much hurt is in his wife's past; he thinks she's frigid, not realizing she's been paralyzed by hurt and shame—and he ends up paying for it.

The irony is, an abused woman often runs to marriage specifically as an excuse to say no to sex. She knows her husband isn't going to use and abuse her, so she gladly accepts the offer of marriage, thinking that once she's in the safe confines of matrimony, she can kiss sex good-bye. The sad fact in all this is that the man who really loves a woman like this is the one who winds up getting stiffed. (We'll talk more about this in a moment, but if you have abuse in your past, I recommend reading Dr. Dan Allender's *The Wounded Heart*, which I think is the best book out there on this subject. Another book every woman needs to read is *Intimate Issues* by Linda Dillow.)

Whatever the case, know this: You have been profoundly shaped, particularly by your opposite-sex parent. If a woman's father abuses her—sexually or otherwise—she's going to have a very difficult time opening up sexually to her husband, even though she may have been sexually promiscuous with many boyfriends. If, on the other hand, she had a very healthy relationship with her father, she is likely going to have less trouble achieving orgasm, and she will tend to have far fewer inhibitions in bed. Fully giving herself to her husband will feel natural and safe.

A man who lived with a domineering and controlling mother may dislike a sexually aggressive wife. A man who found gentle love with his mom, and who was taught to respect her, generally won't have too much trouble becoming sexually intimate with his wife.

Birth order

Your rulebook is also a product of your birth order. If you were in my office, I'd begin asking you questions about your siblings. If you're like Andy, the man who needs to be in control, I'd be willing to wager that you're a firstborn or only-born child. If you think sex and fun should go together most of the time, I'm guessing you're a lastborn child. If you often accommodate your spouse but rarely if ever initiate sex, it wouldn't surprise me at all if you're a middle-born son or daughter.

I deal with birth order extensively in *The New Birth Order Book*, so I'll just summarize here. Lastborns grow up with a tremendous, unflagging sense of entitlement. Because they are often coddled and babied—not just by Mom and Dad, but also often by older siblings—lastborns usually grow up to be "people persons." They are charming, frequently very funny, and often blatant show-offs, loving to be the life of the party. They can also be manipulative, however. Lastborns tend to love surprises, and they are far more open to risks than their older siblings.

In bed, this often results in a desire for surprise, spontaneity, and fun. Lastborns will generally be fairly affectionate but will like to be coddled and taken care of. You better show lastborn spouses a good bit of attention!

Middleborn children are more of a mystery. We don't have time to go into why this is so, but middleborns are the hardest to define, because middle children can go in any number of directions (most often, that direction is directly opposite of the child that is just above them). In general, however, middles like peace at all costs. They are the negotiators, the mediators, and the compromisers. They aren't usually as assertive as firstborn children, but they also require less "care and feeding" than a lastborn child. They will be more secretive and often unselfish to a fault. You may have a hard time getting a middle child to actually tell you what he or she would like in bed.

Firstborns (as well as only children) are the class presidents, the high achievers, the ones who like to be in control and who are convinced that they know the way everything should be done. They are known for being capable and dependable, but they are also perfectionists who are exacting and exhaustingly logical. Their desire for control can lead some to be power mongers and others to be pleasers. If you have sex with the former, you'll feel like you have to jump through hoops to get everything just right—as he or she defines it. If you are married to the latter, this spouse will go out of his or her way to make sure you feel good—but the approach may soon feel mechanical and forced.

There are all kinds of exceptions, but in general, you can learn a good deal about yourself and your spouse by considering your birth order—and how that order of birth has shaped your expectations and your sexual rulebook.

Early memories

The last determiner of your rulebook that we will talk about consists of your early childhood memories.[6] Those early events (when you were in third grade or younger) helped shape your expectations about life and about the way things should be done. You learned either that the world is a safe place . . . or a dangerous place. You developed the assumption that people will either treat you with kindness . . . or betray you and threaten you. Because of what was done to you, you have learned to make any number of assumptions that you now take for granted, and you view your spouse through the lens of these memories.

Here's a case in point: A father promises his young daughter that he will take her out for ice cream after he gets back from the hardware store. The daughter waits by the door for two hours. Eventually Dad does come home, but he smells like alcohol and his speech is slurred. Of course, he forgets all about his promise to take her out for ice cream.

Twenty years later, her husband promises to take her out for dinner. He is legitimately delayed when he gets a flat tire

---

[6]For more information, see *Unlocking the Secrets of Your Childhood Memories* by Dr. Kevin Leman and Randy Carlson (Nashville: Thomas Nelson, 1989).

on the way home. When he does finally show up forty-five minutes late, his wife reads him the riot act. He can't understand why she is so upset because he doesn't realize she's not just yelling at him—she's yelling at her drunken father.

The key is to recognize your tendencies based on your past history and gain a better understanding of these unspoken assumptions. Until you know what they are, you won't be able to edit them.

Editing Your Rulebook

As a speaker who is on the road more weekends than not, I've gone through my share of luggage, and then some. I used to have one suitcase with literally dozens of luggage tags. You see, the airlines ask you to write your name and address on this thin piece of cardboard, which you attach to your bag with an elastic string. The problem is, the tag is so thin and fragile that it usually lasts just two or three flights before it gets torn off. I never removed the torn-off parts; instead, I just attached a new tag. So after a couple years, I must have had fifty or more little pieces of paper tied to the handle—which made the piece of luggage look really ratty and beat-up.

When you look at people's lives like I do, you find that many people are the same way. Their "trips" throughout life have left marks—and not always positive ones. They've been beaten up and are weighed down by their past travels, and over time, they really start to look ratty.

The problem comes in retracing those travels when you only have snippets of information! I've always marveled at electricians, who can open up an electronic device and sort through about fifty different colors of wire. Me? I see red and black, and that's about it. Red means positive, black means negative, and anything else is over my head!

But wading through a person's past is sort of like trying to find an electrical short in the midst of hundreds of wires:

Where did *that* fear come from? What left *that* scar? What created *that* expectation?

So many people's lives have many broken relationships that have left behind psychological scar tissue. Sometimes surgeons have to go in and remove scar tissue because it builds up so much, and in a way, psychologists need to do the same thing. If your cache of scar tissue is particularly deep, you'll need to talk to a professional—but even so, I think this section will help point you in the right direction and get you started asking the right questions.

The good news is, you *can* edit your rulebook. The bad news is, doing so can be difficult and can take a great deal of time. As I just stated, if you've experienced severe trauma—sexual abuse, for instance—you're going to need a professional therapist to help you overcome these early memories and tragic negative parental influence. But many of you can make improvements through making small choices.

First, once you understand your rulebook, remind yourself that just because something feels comfortable to you doesn't make that the standard. A spontaneous man needs to learn that his wife may feel threatened by his spontaneity. Conversely, a controlling woman needs to understand that her lack of spontaneity may be boring her husband right into the arms of another woman. The way you look at sex is the way *you* look at sex—but that doesn't make it the right way, or the only way to look at sex. I'm not saying there aren't any moral absolutes; I certainly believe there are. But I am saying that what we feel about sex within the context of marriage can be a very individual thing.

Here's a secret we'll discuss more thoroughly later in the book, but it's relevant to bring up here: Good lovers learn to know their lover better than they know themselves. You've got to stop viewing sex through your perception alone and start viewing it through your spouse's eyes. If you can do that—understanding your spouse's rulebook in the process—just about everything else we discuss in this book will fall into place. Great marital sex is about learning to love someone else *the way he or she wants to be loved.*

Second, decide that you no longer want to let a parent's shortcomings affect your marital sex life. Think about your inclinations and those areas in the bedroom where you know you fall short, and ask yourself, *Is this what I truly want to give my spouse? Or does he (or she) deserve more?* You then consciously begin practicing the very trait you hope to acquire. The woman who needs the towel under her should try to experience a quickie in the kitchen, just for once. The man who thinks he needs to be in control should let his wife take over one time. When you do this, you will certainly discover that the world doesn't stop turning because you "broke a rule." Your mom will not call you up from the grave and lecture you, "Why didn't you get out a towel?" Your childhood pastor will not suddenly appear in your kitchen wanting to know why the two of you tried *that* sexual position. In fact, you may even find that breaking the rule led to one of the most enjoyable sexual encounters you've had in a long time!

This is something *you* have to initiate. Your spouse can't rewrite your rulebook; you have to do that. You must be the one who discovers it, evaluates it, and then makes a plan to change it. Be honest but firm with yourself: *I know this makes me feel uncomfortable. But even more than my comfort, I value Phil's happiness, so just this once I'm going to see if I can make myself get a little more adventurous.*

Finally, you've got to put away the past. The only way I know how to help someone do that is to reconnect with the power of God in their life. If we ask for forgiveness, God will remove the stain of our sin and forgive us, leaving us psychologically fresh and new.

This is a spiritual reality I've seen happen time and time

again. As much as some of my colleagues like to belittle Christianity and religious faith in general, I have found it to be the most powerful method of dealing with past hurts, sins, and psychological scar tissue. Don't get me wrong: I'm not a Christian because Christianity *works*. I'm a Christian because I believe Christianity is true—but the fact that it also works very well has served my clients and me greatly.

If you really want to start anew, you need to align yourself with God's principles. That means, first, if you're living together but not married, you need to find separate living arrangements. Start to date again, but keep sex out of your relationship.

As much as this is the moral thing to do, it's also the right thing to do, psychologically speaking. By now, just about everyone has heard the phrase "recycled virgins"—people who were once sexually promiscuous (sexually active, for our politically correct friends) but who have now made the choice to abstain until marriage. This is a very healthy model for those who have lost their initial virginity to follow. For their own sake, these couples need to see God making a change in their lives in order to build a stronger foundation for their marriage. They need to experience not just God's forgiveness, but also the power he provides to help us resist temptation.

Why is this so important? Let me put it this way: Your marriage's chances of survival are based on you and your spouse's level of self-control. I once counseled a young couple to stop having sex until after they got married, and the young man casually replied, "I don't know if I can make it for three or four months without having sex. If Sheila and I stop having sex, I might be tempted to look for it elsewhere."

Without blinking, I turned to the young woman and said, "If he can't keep his hands off you or any other woman for three months because he lacks the discipline, what possible hope is there after you get married and he's off on business five days a week while you're at home surrounded by little kids?"

The things God asks us to do as single men and women are the very things that build in us the character qualities we need as husbands and wives. If we short-circuit the process, we cheat ourselves, and we enter marriage inadequately prepared for a happy, long-lasting relationship. The more couples I talk to, the more convinced I become that God knew what he was talking about when he prescribed no sex before marriage, and lots of great sex after marriage.

Beyond all this, there really is a tremendous cleansing power in knowing that God has forgiven you for what you've done. Having said this, I also need to gently remind you that while God removes the stain, he doesn't always remove the consequences. The reality, for many of you, is that even though you've been forgiven, you must become like the alcoholic whose credo is "one day at a time." You've damaged your soul by giving your body to many lovers, and that means you'll need some emotional, spiritual, and relational therapy.

Like everything in life, you'll need to build on some small successes. If you have flashbacks of former sexual partners, you'll need to learn on a case-by-case basis how to turn your attention back to your spouse (more on this in a moment). You garner strength when you learn to say no when you want to say yes. The more you do this, the stronger you become, and the more self-control you gain.

A disciplined life is a joyful life, because when you internalize boundaries you protect yourself from the very things that will bring the most pain into your life and marriage and sexual bed. Imagine being wrapped up in passion with your spouse, and suddenly someone else comes to mind, marring what had been a very special session of lovemaking.

That's the shame of it all. A sexual track record tends to follow us. Some people have so much baggage tattered to their psychological and sexual self, so many little name tags that have never been completely torn off, that it gets very difficult

not to compare this man or woman you deeply love and respect to some hot little number you wrestled with many a
night years ago.

Since this has, unfortunately, become so prevalent in our
society, let's talk more about dealing with your sexual past.

YOUR SEXUAL PAST: FIGHTING FLASHBACKS

I wish I could say that if you've been sexually active, don't
worry—you can be just like a virgin again. But if I said that, I'd
be lying. God will forgive you, your spouse can accept you.
But it's far healthier to be realistic if you've had previous sexual experience. A recycled virgin still brings more baggage to
the marriage bed than a true virgin. There's a reason God tells
us to save sex until marriage, and there are consequences if we
step over that line.

For starters, you may have flashbacks. Sexual memories are a
natural phenomenon if you've had other lovers in your life.
Unfortunately, these flashbacks can interfere with a healthy
marital sex life. I've had several patients confide that flashbacks
were a significant problem, particularly those who had a strict
upbringing and who didn't live up to it. For women, the guilt
can feel almost overwhelming at times. They're making love to
their husband when suddenly ex-boyfriend Richard comes to
mind. Since sex is such an emotional experience for women, a
flashback robs them of the meaning and the moment.

Men, on the other hand, tend to compare the physical reactions, and their flashbacks are more likely based on comparison. What if a former girlfriend knew how to touch you in a
particularly satisfying way? And what if your wife is worried
that she'll never be able to compete? And when she asks you
about it, she can tell that, so far, she hasn't come close to
pleasing you like that other woman used to? The pain of such
a realization cuts very deeply. Men who have previous sexual

experiences may also have a hard time valuing the emotional connection of married sex since they're focused more specifically on physical pleasure.

It's not easy, but you've got to start anew, and that means letting your spouse start anew as well. Remember what we talked about in the previous section: Once you've asked for forgiveness, God has forgiven you. I realize it's easy to have that understanding but not always quite so easy to accept it emotionally. If I knew how to keep the thoughts away, I wouldn't be a psychologist; I'd be a magician! The things we want to repress and not think about are usually the things that pop up in our minds during the most inappropriate times.

Here's a little trick: As soon as you get that memory, start talking to your husband, saying how much you love him, how much you want to please him, what he means to you, or how aroused you feel. If the latter isn't true, take his hands and help him please you so that all of your conscious thoughts and words are focused on him instead of thinking of another.

In other words, your assignment is to relearn how to have the best sex possible with your spouse. Whenever any memories intrude on your current sex life, try to make your present sex life that much more satisfying. You get rid of the old by focusing on the new. This is a conscious choice: *I'm not going to dwell on that memory; instead, I'm going to daydream about how to make my spouse cry out with pleasure.*

How well this works will depend in part on how much damage has been done. You can get away with not brushing your teeth once in a while, but if you neglect your teeth for months or years on end, you're going to get gum disease. If, at the first onset of that disease, you suddenly decide to become the best flosser in the neighborhood and start brushing your teeth after every meal, you may be able to prevent further infection, but you're still going to have to recover from the previous damage.

It's like a smoker who quits. As a former smoker myself, I

know I'm much healthier now that I haven't lit up in over thirty-five years. But while I'm much healthier for quitting, I'd still be better off if I had never smoked a single cigarette in the first place.

TO SHARE OR NOT TO SHARE?

When dealing with a couple's sexual past, the first question that usually comes up in the counseling room is, "How much of our past should we share?"

My answer is, "As little as possible."

Your spouse deserves to know whether he or she is marrying a virgin; he or she also has a right to know whether you've slept with just one boyfriend or girlfriend, or whether your promiscuity put you in bed with multiple partners. Your spouse has a right to know this because it may affect whether or not he or she decides to marry you—and rightly so.

But going into specifics causes far more problems than it solves. Generally speaking, *don't share past sexual secrets*. All this does is raise insecurity; suddenly the conversation switches from "I want to know everything about you" to something much, much uglier: "What do you mean you did it three times in one night?" "I thought the hot tub idea was ours!" Listen, if God wanted us to understand what everyone was thinking, he would have given us glass foreheads. It is a gift to your spouse to let some memories die in the past and remain only with you.

A far healthier approach is to simply confess, "Listen, honey, there are some things in my past that I just wish weren't there" and leave it at that. Sharing any details ("We didn't have intercourse, but we did get a little carried away one night and . . .") is just flat-out asking for trouble. Simply confess, "You're not marrying a virgin. I truly wish you were, but you're not."

If a partner presses, use me as an excuse: "A counselor I

know suggests that the healthiest thing is for both of us to realize that we are marrying imperfect people with imperfect pasts. Let's start from the ground up and build the best marriage possible, knowing that from this point on, sex is something that will be shared exclusively with each other—and I want to give you the best sex life possible."

Then I recommend that you spend considerable time talking about how wonderful it's going to be when you're finally married. Below is a letter a young woman wrote to her fiancé just six weeks before they got married. He had sexual experience but she didn't, and she sensed he was nervous about whether she would be sexually responsive in marriage, especially since she was usually the one putting her foot down about going too far.

What's so wonderful about this letter is the way the young woman helps her husband-to-be wait for sexual intimacy while she builds expectation for their marriage bed:

Dear husband-to-be,

Happy anniversary! Do you realize we met exactly two years ago today? I have to confess that I never believed I could meet a man with whom I feel so completely comfortable as I do with you. For years I struggled with the thought that someday I would have to be married because that's the thing to do. I've never told anybody this, but I never could really understand why anybody would even want to have sex with a guy—until I met you. Now it's all I can do to keep my hands off your body!

You have brought out and reawakened every

feminine quality that I had buried in the depth of my heart. You have made me want to be the woman I've become today. When you look at me with that impish grin, you make my heart smile and flutter. I practically melt from loving you and wanting you so much.

Six weeks from today, I'll be your wife. In this day and age, where everybody has to "find themselves," I can't wait to be a part of you. The thought of being your wife makes me excited and proud. What makes it even extra special is that you've really worked hard at keeping us pure. I don't think I've ever really told you this, but it's very hard for me not to want to touch you all over. I'll admit it: sometimes I find myself day dreaming about being totally naked, wrapped up in your arms, and we are all over each other.

Just think, we've only got six more weeks of waiting and that dream will come true! Just so you know, I don't plan to hold anything back, so I hope you're ready!

But I do thank you from the bottom of my heart for being so disciplined and loving me the way you love me so we can start off our marriage with as positive and healthy a start as possible. I can't tell you how much your love means to me, and how you've changed my entire outlook on life. I never could imagine wanting to give myself to a man the *way I want to give myself to you (you ought to be smiling right now as you read this note). I love you totally.*

Yours forever,
Anne

What a wonderful letter and a great example of how a woman can tell a future husband who is getting a little impatient how eager she is to explore the delights of sexual intimacy, while also reinforcing how important it is to wait.

Some of you married readers may have realized that, because of your rulebook or your sexual past, you've withheld a part of yourself from your spouse. You haven't given your body to your spouse the way this woman is promising to give herself to her future husband. Maybe you've been accommodating but not eager. You know you're not putting in the time and energy your husband or wife deserves. You've let your sexual intimacy wane, and frankly, you've taken your spouse's commitment and fidelity for granted.

May I suggest you write a similar letter? Decide what you've been holding back, ask your spouse's forgiveness, and then tell him or her what you hope to do. Don't let your past dictate your future. Your Creator wants you to have a thrilling and fulfilling sex life. With his forgiveness and a little work on your end to face your past squarely, you *can* change your rulebook. You *can* become the type of lover you want to be and you know your spouse deserves.

What are you waiting for?

3

Shake, Rattle, and Roll!

Why a Good Sex Life Is Worth Striving For

Tell me something: What would the movie *Jaws* be like without that menacing music? Ba-*dum,* ba-*dum,* ba-*dum,* ba-*dum.* Think it would be half as scary?

I don't.

Imagine *Star Wars* with no triumphant composition playing as Luke Skywalker defeats the Death Star and saves the galaxy. I don't think it would be nearly as exciting, do you?

Or try to imagine those guys running for the gold medals in *Chariots of Fire.* Watching people run in slow motion without music to set the scene wouldn't be a good recipe for an Oscar in my book.

Each one of these blockbuster movies had a good script, good actors, and a very competent director—but none of them would be the same without the music. The music alone wouldn't be enough, of course, but music is still a vital and essential element for a hit movie.

Sex is that way for marriage. You can be married without having any sex at all. You can still talk over dinner, celebrate the holidays, and—if you adopt—raise children. You can buy each other anniversary gifts, share intimate conversations, and even, in an emergency, share toothbrushes or bring in an urgently needed roll of toilet paper.

But something would still be missing.

A good sex life colors the marriage from top to bottom. Life requires us to do a lot of humdrum things. Sometimes my wife needs me to go to the store and pick up a bunch of boring stuff—lettuce, celery, lightbulbs, milk, ho-hum. But other times, I get to go to a lingerie store and buy something that's anything but boring.

At other times Sande needs me to find out why the brakes squeak and squawk and make all kinds of nasty noises when she's driving the car. But in even better times, I get to discover what makes my wife squeak and squawk and moan and groan!

On some occasions Sande wants me to take out the Christmas decorations (and then, believe it or not, she expects me to put them back just six weeks later!) or take out the garbage. But in even better times, I get to take down the clothes she's wearing. I love that job!

Think about it: 90 percent of life is filled with mostly boring stuff, like changing dirty diapers, cleaning up countless spills, paying the bills, filling the gas tank. And many men and women often have to work in deadly dull jobs—checking food at the grocery store, pounding nails into a roof, or adding up the same batch of figures. I've even met accomplished lawyers and dentists who were bored out of their minds with their professions, but financial obligations insisted that they keep doing them.

Into this world of obligation and responsibility, God has

dropped something absolutely fabulous into our laps. At the end of the day (and sometimes at the beginning!), when our work is done and the kids are in bed and we're home from work, we can touch each other and kiss each other and pleasure each other in such a way that the world feels like it is light-years away. We're transported to another place and removed to another time, and it's a glorious feeling indeed.

A fulfilling sex life is one of the most powerful marital glues a couple can have. Children are a powerful "glue," as are common values, a common faith, and common dreams. But sex is definitely one of the strongest.

The kind of sex I'm talking about takes a little work and a lot of forethought—but the dividends it pays are more than worth the effort. If your husband is sexually fulfilled, he'll do anything for you. He'll take a bullet, he'll race a train, and he'll do whatever it takes to make sure you're okay. And men, if your wife knows that you view sex as a special gift to give to her; if you can make your wife feel things she's never felt before; and if you will learn to become a selfless, sensitive, and competent lover, she'll purr like a kitten and melt in your arms.

A sexually fulfilled man will normally be a better father and a better employee. A sexually fulfilled woman will have less stress and more joy in her life. Sex is vitally important to a healthy marriage.

DIFFERENT INSTRUMENTS

Have you ever heard a small child learn to play the piano? Probably everyone has heard the obnoxious "Chopsticks" that first-time students learn, but most beginning songs are usually played one note at a time. When the child becomes more advanced, she learns to play chords; she begins using two hands, and two hands make all the difference. The kind of music you can produce with two hands is many hundred times more beautiful than what you can create with one hand.

Again, the same principle is true of sex. A man and a woman are the two hands of sex as God designed it. Neither one is the same; neither "hand" will play the same notes. But when they're working in tandem, they can create some of the most beautiful sounds ever heard.

What I want for you as a couple is to have two people who are sexually fulfilled. A wife or husband who has sex only out of duty will not fulfill his or her partner. Yes, there are times when sex will feel like a duty—at least initially—but if it *always* feels like a duty, it's not fulfilling in the sense I'm talking about.

Since sex does take some work, let me tell you why it's *worth* the work. Let me speak first to the wives. Here is why it's to your benefit to have a sexually fulfilled husband.

Women: Why You Want to Make Hubby Happy

1. A sexually fulfilled husband will do anything for you.
Sex is such a basic need for men that when this area of their life is well taken care of, they feel immense appreciation and act accordingly. A sexually fulfilled man is the kind who drives to work thinking, *I'm so glad I married that woman. I must be the happiest man alive!* And who then drives home thinking, *What special thing can I do for my wife this evening?* If you want this kind of loyalty and appreciation, meet your husband's sexual needs; no other needs generate such deep thankfulness. Instead of resenting requests to stop by the store or take a look at a leaky faucet, a sexually fulfilled man will jump with eagerness. Instead of being cold and distant when you talk to him, he's going to want to hear what you have to say.

Some wives reading this may be thinking, *I tried that, and it didn't work.* Such a response shows me that you're misunderstanding me entirely. You can't just "try" this; it has to become a way of life. One good time of sex will make a man thankful—for a while. But if he's turned down the next five times he approaches you, he'll think about the five rejections, not that one special night.

Because of a man's chemical makeup, sex feels like a need to most of us, and when a woman graciously and eagerly meets that need, we become very thankful. When a woman uses a man's need to manipulate him, a man becomes resentful. When a woman uses a man's need to punish him, he often becomes bitter.

For the majority of men, this sexual need is the primary request that they seek from their wives. You can be the best cook, a great mother, and a fantastic conversationalist, but if you put no thought or effort into your lovemaking, your husband will probably feel disappointed. Conversely, if you give your husband a thrilling sex life, you might be surprised at how little he cares about other things that go wanting.

2. A sexually fulfilled husband is a scriptural mandate.

One time, late at night, Sande asked me to read the Bible to her. "Sure, honey," I said. "I'd love to."

She was a little surprised by my eagerness, but hey, I have an obligation to be the spiritual leader, don't I? I wanted to take my role seriously.

I flipped open my Bible to 1 Corinthians 7:3-5: "The husband should fulfill his marital duty to his wife, and likewise the wife to her husband. The wife's body does not belong to her alone but also to her husband. In the same way, the husband's body does not belong to him alone but also to his wife. Do not deprive each other except by mutual consent and for a time, so that you may devote yourselves to prayer. Then come together again so that Satan will not tempt you because of your lack of self-control" (NIV).

If you call yourself a Christian, and if you're committed to being obedient to what the Bible teaches, then you'll have to learn to fulfill sexual obligations within marriage. I don't pretend to be a Bible scholar, but this passage is clear enough that I can give you the Leman translation: One thing Paul is telling us is he wants us to do it. And if we want to stop for prayer, that's okay. And then what I love about this great saint of the church is that he wants us to do it again!

C. K. Barrett's translation is just as strong. Instead of the somewhat polite "do not deprive each other" put forward by the New International Version above, Barrett translates the Greek, "Do not *rob* one another."[7] Now, men can rob women as well as vice versa; the obligation is on both parties. But the bottom line is this: to say to your spouse, "The store is closed," or even, "You can shop on this shelf, but not that shelf" is less than Christian.

Now, if talking to your husband, I would remind him that one of the all-time great biblical lines is "Love does not demand its own way" (1 Corinthians 13:5). When a guy tries to use 1 Corinthians 7 to get his wife to do something kinky or distasteful to her ("Honey, you have to have anal sex if I want it" or, "You have to swallow"), give me a break! That's *not* what Paul is talking about. Just as Paul tells us we have sexual obligations within marriage, in the same book he insists that love does not demand its own way. In short, men, you don't force, *ever*.

Marriage is an exercise in mutual submission. We need to be realistic, of course. Admittedly, there are times when my head hits the pillow at night, thinking sex, and Sande's head hits the pillow, also thinking sex, but both of us wake up the next morning and realize that nothing has happened. Yes, there are times where you're too pooped to whoop; but if you're the *only* one too pooped, you may be willing to whoop anyway because you know doing so will please your spouse.

What I like so much about 1 Corinthians 7 is that Paul

---

[7]C. K. Barrett, *A Commentary on the First Epistle to the Corinthians, Second Edition* (London: Adam and Charles Black, 1971), 156.

completely removes the religious argument (as if someone could use God to avoid sex) and turns it around, saying to married couples, "If you truly love God, you'll have sex!"

I can be very direct with spouses when I'm talking about this. If you really love your spouse and he or she, to put it bluntly, really wants your body, you're being selfish if you withhold it. That's not to say we're never selfish, because all of us are from time to time, but you can't make a marriage grow from a selfish attitude for a long period of time. Eventually your selfishness will kill it.

A wife who is in tune with her husband's needs and desires can really help him live a holy life. While writing this book I talked to one couple in which the husband had struggled for many years with an addiction to pornography. Although pornography is connected to deeper issues—isolation, loneliness, the inability to connect with others emotionally, to name a few—it can be an additional struggle for a man if his wife either isn't interested in, or available for, sex. The most difficult time for this man was during his wife's period, because she was unavailable to him sexually. After about ten years, she finally realized that pleasing her husband with oral sex or a simple "hand job" did wonders to help her husband through that difficult time. She realized that faithfulness is a two-person job. That doesn't mean a husband can escape the blame for using pornography by pointing to an uncooperative wife—we all make our own choices—but a wife can make it much easier for her husband to maintain a pure mind.

Here's a common scenario: A husband wakes up early in the morning with incontrovertible physical evidence that Mr. Happy is more than ready to go "dancing." He looks over and there's his wife, sleeping tenderly. With a quick glance at the clock, he notices that it's 6:15 and they don't have to get up until 7:00.

The more he thinks about it, the more intriguing the

thought of sex becomes. *Forty-five minutes!* he says to himself. *Man, what I could do in forty-five minutes!*

He then starts to communicate in a way that only a man would think effective—he reaches his toe over to his wife's side of the bed and pokes her, hoping she'll get the hint. When that doesn't work, he might become more direct and grab a breast, fully expecting, even after fifteen years of marriage, mind you, that this grab will turn her into a raging sex kitten: "Why honey, I was waiting all night for you to wake me up by grabbing a handful of my breasts!" Or—my favorite—he'll look at a woman who has both eyes closed and who is snoring like a donkey and loudly ask, "Honey, are you asleep?"

Every man has his own protocol, but more often than not it'll take just three or four annoying little pokes or prods before the wife rears back like a horse with a burr under its saddle screaming, "What do you think you're doing?! I still have forty-five minutes left to sleep!"

Sometimes the wife will be less forceful. "I haven't even brushed my teeth yet. Surely you don't want to kiss me!"

Honey, he wants to do a whole lot more than kiss!

If the marriage is a selfish one, the man will hear all sorts of defenses: "We'll wake the children." "I'm tired." "Are you some kind of a sex addict?"

If the marriage is a selfless but nonfulfilling one, the wife may acquiesce with a few stipulations and all the enthusiasm of someone reading the phone book. She becomes a sexual receptacle, but that's about it.

If the marriage is a satisfied one, both parties will see the other's side. The man may realize his wife needs her sleep and, because of his love for her, let her get that sleep—only to pursue her sexually later. Or the wife may sacrificially decide that giving her body, with joy, to her husband is more important than those extra few minutes of precious sleep—because of the benefits to their relationship.

Some of these interludes, although they may start off rocky, can really end up being great, if there's enough time to get things going. But in so many marriages, when a spouse gets turned down, the seeds of bitterness are planted in the relationship to the point where, later that day, the wife asks the husband to take her mother grocery shopping and he says, "No, I can't."

"Why not? You're just watching the game."

"I'm busy."

"You don't look busy."

"I don't care what I look like, I'm busy. If your mom needs to go shopping, why don't you take her?"

What's going on here?

It's a delayed reaction. Admittedly, it's a cheap shot, but it happens all the time. The husband thinks to himself, *If she turns me down, I'll turn her down.*

Proverbs 13:12 tells us, "Hope deferred makes the heart sick." Tell me, what was the hope for your marriage? What did you think it would be like? What do you think your spouse hoped for? If those hopes are discarded without thought, eventually a spouse's heart becomes sick. I've seen this happen over and over again: Young, happily married couples slowly watch a once-happy affection get completely buried by steady shovelfuls of bitterness and resentment. They become petty instead of kind, self-seeking instead of generous. And frankly, they make each other miserable.

When a man's hopes are regularly beaten down, anger, hostility, and resentment will eventually fill that house. Certainly, a lot of us have unrealistic hopes that need to be challenged—quite frankly, I thought I'd have sex every night of my marriage, and it didn't take me too many nights to figure out that wasn't going to happen! That's why it's so important to talk about your expectations and hopes with your spouse—before your marriage, at the beginning of your marriage, and all throughout your marriage. It's the only way to find out, for you as a couple, which needs are unrealistic, and which are legitimate. Hopes that are legitimate shouldn't be simply tossed aside; if they sour, they'll infect every aspect of your relationship.

3. A sexually fulfilled husband will feel good about himself.

So much of who we are as men is tied up in how our wives respond to us sexually. While this may surprise some of you wives, as a psychologist I believe that every healthy man wants to be his wife's hero. He wants to be like the late, great conductor Arthur Fiedler, leading his wife to a crescendo of ecstasy. While he's delighted that you're experiencing an ecstatic orgasm, he's also watching you thinking, *I did that to her, thank you very much.*

He may not be the top dog at work, he may not have the fastest car, he may be losing what little looks he had to begin with, his hair may be falling out while his gut is getting bigger, but if his honey loves him enough to occasionally put a few scratches on his back in the heat of passion, he will still feel like the king of the world. Why? Because he can please his woman. There isn't a husband on this planet who doesn't want to know he can make his woman go crazy in bed.

Conversely, if you want to emasculate a man, the bedroom is certainly the best place to do it. Call him a sex addict. Ridicule his lovemaking skills. Act like there's nothing he could do to turn you on. But if you do this, watch out. He'll find a way to strike back at you. Yes—he'll find a way. Believe me.

4. A sexually fulfilled husband will take on his life work with a vigor and purpose that is unmatched.

In today's climate of downsizing and fear of losing your job, a fulfilling sex life is sort of like putting your husband on a rechargeable battery. Every time the two of you have sex, and your husband knows you desire him physically, it recharges his battery. He'll take on the world, or that troublesome boss, or that difficult vocational challenge, or that seemingly closed job market, one more time. Twenty firms may have rejected him, but if the man has a loving wife at home, he'll wake up the next day to visit twenty more.

Sex is energizing for a man. It builds confidence in him and creates an overall sense of well-being. He garners strength to persevere in an unfulfilling job because he is tuned in to those he loves—there's a purpose for his working, and a reward at the end of the day.

Men get a great deal of satisfaction from providing for their families. Of course, in this day and age the great majority of women also work outside the home, but I don't think women get the same psychological jollies from bringing home a paycheck as most men do. Sure, a few women do—but most see outside work as a necessary effort on their part to help the family.

5. A sexually fulfilled husband appreciates the important things in life.

Men are one of two things: home-centered or outside-the-home-centered. The outside-the-home-centered man may find his satisfaction by working long hours, or by going out to taverns and drinking with his buddies. Some may even escape to church. But whether a man is going to an office, a bar, or a church, if he's leaving his wife and kids at home, he's centered outside the home.

If a man is home-centered, it's likely because the queen is keeping the king pretty happy. A man's place is in the home. Many years ago people often said a woman's place is in the home. Women took great offense, but I think men belong there every bit as much as women! A man may have many bosses outside the home, but inside the home, he has the opportunity to kindly provide authority and to receive his rightful respect. A good home is a place every healthy man needs.

My travels often require me to be away from home, but I'm very home-centered. I can't wait to get home, and when I'm away from home, I call so often that I sometimes drive Sande crazy. "Look, Lemey," she says, "you may be on the road, but I've got to get a little work done around here!" A dream day for me is to be at home, putzing around the house with nothing to do. I just love it there. I can't even imagine wanting to be anywhere else.

If a man is centered on something outside the home, he'll always have to leave home to get his batteries recharged. He will come home only reluctantly, and when he is home, his mind will be somewhere else. He'll act like he resents being home, and he'll grow short with people who "bother" him while he's at home. His wife and kids will get just the scraps, not the prime cuts.

If a man is home-centered—in large part because at home he feels like he's loved, wanted, and accepted for who he is, and he has a wife who wants to please him—he'll do anything that will strengthen the home because that's his most important world. He won't think twice about sacrificing prestige at the office to be home by dinner; he won't let a boss browbeat him into missing his son's ball games or get home too late to tuck the kids into bed. He'll make sure the house gets repaired, because a healthy home is important to him—more important than anything else except, perhaps, his faith.

Some of you wives may be reading this thinking, *Why isn't my husband home-centered?* You want to blame him, but let me turn the tables: Are you sexually pursuing him? Does he have reason to believe that his sexual needs and desires will be met in creative and sometimes spontaneous ways? In other words, are you making home a more exciting place to come back to?

If you are, your husband will want to make the investment of time and energy so you are sexually fulfilled.

Men: Making Your Wife Purr

1. It's better to watch.

Let's face it, men—our most natural fallen state tempts us to become voyeurs. That's our gender bent, so to speak. Men purchase the overwhelming majority of pornography. Women rarely call 1-900 numbers and pay three dollars a minute to hear a man talk dirty to them. Why?

Men like to watch.

There's a healthy side to this, however. We were made to watch *one woman in particular,* not all women in general. Our Creator wired us in such a way that we become just as thrilled watching our wife reach orgasm as we do reaching orgasm ourselves. That's why pornography or prostitution will never satisfy a man's soul. Most men feel demeaned and ashamed after a solitary sexual experience—in our heart of hearts, we don't just want to *be* satisfied, we want to satisfy our wives. The best satisfaction comes from satisfying someone else, not in being satisfied. And that's something pornography, phone sex, lap dances, or prostitution can never give you.

If you've fallen into the gutter of any type of porn, put all that time, effort, and expense into creating a satisfying sexual relationship with your wife. Learn to enjoy sex by watching your wife have the time of her life.

"But Dr. Leman," some men have protested, "you don't understand. Talking about my wife's sexual needs is an oxymoron—she doesn't have any!"

In a later chapter we'll discuss the problem of low libido on the part of both men and women, but for now, let me suggest just one possibility: Have you approached sex as something you deserve and want, or have you approached sex as a very wonderful way to please your wife like no other man can?

It may be that your wife has no interest in sex the way *you* want to have it. But are you sure she doesn't want to have sex in a different way? Have you ever considered the fact that if you finished up the dishes and put the kids to bed while she soaked in a hot tub, and then you rubbed some lotion into her feet when she got out and maybe read to her or talked to her about her day, that's what sex means to her? And buddy, I'm not talking about doing this just one time, expecting one night out of a thousand to turn your wife around sexually! This needs to become a way of life before your wife will feel rested enough and appreciative enough to open up more sexually.

Learn to find *your* satisfaction in your wife's orgasm, and you'll change your love life. Instead of making sex something you demand, try to make it something you offer. To truly offer something that's inviting, you've got to make it look enticing *to your wife.* Find out what gets her purring, and pursue that.

2. Who's winning the marriage?

Sometimes when a couple sits down in my office, they erupt into an immediate catfight. I'll let them go on just long enough to make my point, then I'll ask, "Tell me, who is winning the marriage?"

At times I'll be met with a confused stare: *What is this guy talking about?* But most often, the couples will know what I'm talking about. What I'm really asking them is, "Who has gained the upper hand?"

I then go on: "If someone is winning this marriage, both of you are losing because marriage is not a sport, it's a relationship."

Control wreaks havoc in a marriage, and control is where most men fail. Because a man is often expected to be the physical aggressor, it's easy for him to develop a controlling position in marriage by being so dominant sexually, "proving" his masculinity every time he has sexual relations.

You know what? Sometimes a woman enjoys being "vanquished," if that taking is in the midst of a healthy, loving, and committed marriage. But I've never met a woman who wants sex to be like that all the time, or even most of the time.

If sex becomes a real problem issue in a marriage, it's often some kind of power struggle over "who's the boss." And men are very adept at the subtle ways that they wield power. In fact, a woman can be "controlled" by a man who never approaches her for sex. In a passive way, he always insists that the wife initiate sexual relations, so he never risks being turned down. In reality, this is an aggressive act of "passive control." She has to come to him *on his terms.* Initially it doesn't appear to be controlling; in fact, it may seem very laid-back. But there is a psychological MO at play: For him to have emotionally satisfying sex, it has to be on his terms with her initiating.

A much healthier model is one of mutual submissiveness. This may be one of the most difficult things I discuss in the counseling room, because mutual submissiveness insists you die to your self, and if there's one thing Americans don't want to give up, it's self. We even have a magazine with *Self* as the title! But marriage is about learning to put someone else's needs above your own, and this goes far beyond the bedroom. It's about graciously doing the mundane, everyday things as part of being a couple, developing a friendship, and caring for each other.

If you "win" your marriage, you'll lose at life. Give up control. Use your authority to serve, protect, and pleasure. That's where it's really at, my friend.

3. Sexually pursue your wife outside the bedroom.

Good sex is an all-day affair.[8] You can't treat your wife like a servant and expect her to be eager to sleep with you at night. Your wife's sexual responsiveness will be determined by how

[8]For further information on this subject, read *Sex Begins in the Kitchen* by Dr. Kevin Leman (Grand Rapids, Mich.: Revell, 1999).

willingly you help out with the dishes, the kids' homework, or that leaky faucet that drips throughout the night.

This is so difficult for many men to understand, in large part because we remove sex from every other part of our life. We think sex fixes things on its own—but it doesn't do that for a woman. The context, the history, the current level of emotional closeness—all that directly affects your wife's desire and enjoyment of sexual relations.

That's why I spend a lot of time trying to help women get more active in the bedroom and trying to help men get more active everywhere else. If we could just meet each other halfway on this, most marriages would do fine. A good lover works just as hard outside the bedroom as he does inside it.

THE MOST TERRIFYING ACT IN THE WORLD

Most men don't realize, psychologically, how vulnerable a naked woman can feel. The very act of sex is one in which she is inviting someone else into her body. You can't get any more intimate than that.

Ask any woman how she feels about going to a gynecologist. Most women I talk to loathe this necessary appointment. Think about how demeaning it would be to visit an invariably cold office and then be asked to strip naked. You're given a flimsy gown to wear with an embarrassing flap in the back, told to put one leg in one stirrup and one in another so that you're spread-eagled, one leg going northeast and one going northwest, and you now feel like your most private parts are on public display as a fully clothed man (or if you're a little luckier, a woman) walks into the room. That's about as vulnerable as it gets.

And, oh yes, they cover you with a thin, white sheet. How nice.

In many ways, marriage can feel like a visit to a gynecologist's office. Marriage asks us to take off all the masks we use to protect ourselves from being hurt. Men fearfully wonder if their wife will ridicule them for their sexual requests; women wonder if their husband will find their bodies desirable. Marriage and marital sexuality require a lot of trust. People who have been hurt by life are going to keep their knees together emotionally.

That's why the marriage bed is usually a pretty accurate picture of what else is going on in the marriage. The degree to which a couple can develop a vulnerability to each other eventually gets played out in the bedroom, for good or for ill. If trust isn't built up, the marital bed will grow colder. When trust is lovingly handled, marital passion usually heats up. Conversely, success in the marital bed usually gets played out somewhere else in the relationship; the wife and husband are kinder to each other and treat each other with greater respect.

When you improve your marriage, you'll usually improve your sex life. When you improve your sex life, you'll usually improve the rest of your marriage. The two are intricately entwined, so making more effort in any one area is a very good investment.

Wives, do you want your husband to be a better father? Do you want him to spend more time at home? Do you want him to listen to you more carefully? If you do, work at helping him become sexually fulfilled.

Husbands, do you want a wife who has less stress, who is more appreciative and respectful of you? Then learn what pleases her sexually.

Every couple can benefit from improving their sex lives. It's very pleasant work, and in my experience, there are few things that produce such amazing fringe benefits.

Learning to Make Music

The First Night and Beyond

4

Confession: I was dumber than mud when I got married. I don't want you to make the same mistakes on your honeymoon that I did. If you're already married, please don't stop reading just yet. If you take the time to do so, you may find that going back to the foundation can really pay big dividends even after twenty or thirty years of marriage.

For starters, I never had a dad who took me aside and told me I should take Sande to a nice romantic place to get engaged. We didn't have any money, and I probably couldn't have afforded a nice romantic place anyway. So I gave Sande her engagement ring in a field behind my parents' house. She accepted my proposal surrounded by ragweed instead of roses.

By the way, on a summer's day in Arizona, snakes rule the grass. "Honey, would you marry me?"

"Sure!"

Slither, slither, chomp, chomp.

I cringe when I think back to our wedding night, when Sande and I first started "doing it." I am so lucky that Sande didn't just lock the door at the Travel Lodge and tell me she'd find her own way home.

Yes, we stayed at a Travel Lodge our first night, but it was a nice Travel Lodge—it cost me twelve dollars a night, plus tax!

You see, nobody told me Jack-Diddly about taking Sande to a luxury hotel. Nobody told me you don't spend the first night of your married life in Yuma, Arizona. Do you know how hot it is on an August night in Yuma, Arizona? It makes hell seem like Buffalo, New York, in January, that's how hot it is.

And nobody said it was wrong to spend the first three days of our honeymoon going to a California Angels–New York Yankees series. I was a big Mickey Mantle fan, and he was coming to the West Coast! Marriage or not, how could you pass that up? Besides, what could be better than baseball during the day and sex every night?

I look back at our honeymoon and cringe, but Sande is sweet about it: "Oh, honey, I loved our honeymoon."

Yeah, right. She loved the three baseball games ("Is this halftime, dear?" "No, honey, it's the seventh-inning stretch."), she loved staying in a hotel that was located conveniently close to the railroad tracks, and I'm sure she particularly appreciated the view—a blinking beer sign that lit up the night sky ("Oh, but honey, I love neon. I really do.").

If you pick up your local Sunday paper and read the wedding notices, you'll hear about couples going to Maui, to Ecuador, or on a cruise to the Caribbean. I defy you to find a single notice that lists going to Yuma, Arizona, and a three-game series between the Angels and the Yankees.

I was dumb as mud. Didn't have a clue. But somehow Sande and I survived. While today's couples tend to be better at planning the location of their honeymoons, I've found that many still lack some basic knowledge about how to get their marriage off to the right start, especially the sexual aspect. Listen to a typical premarital counseling session:

A young couple walks into my office on the day we're scheduled to talk about sex. I hand a violin to the young man and say, "Play this for me, please."

He looks at the violin, looks back at me, and says, "I don't play the violin."

"It's not rocket science. There's the bow, there are the strings. Rub the bow across the strings. I want to hear you play it."

The young man reluctantly takes the bow in hand, runs his arm south, and all three of us flinch at the terrible squeaking noise that erupts from the instrument.

"That's good," I say.

"What do you mean, that's good? It sounded awful."

"For a first attempt, that was good. You made noise. Now here's the problem: We need to make music."

I then hand the violin to the bride. "Let's hear you play it."

She takes the instrument from her fiancé, pushes her arm forward, and makes an equally frightful sound.

"Good," I said. "You can both make noise. The object is to play music. You're both going to experience something in a couple weeks—and you know what I'm talking about. After the wedding, you'll check in at the hotel, maybe even feeling a little naughty. After all, the two of you are going to spend the entire night together. In bed! Behind a locked door!

"But the first night might result in more noise than music; even so, that's no reason to be discouraged. Let's go back to playing the violin. If you really applied yourselves, a good guess is that you'd eventually be able to pick up that violin and actually make people clap when they hear you play. But not right off the bat. Like a musician starting out, you're going to need training and practice.

"Here's your assignment for the honeymoon: Learn all the complexities of each other's strengths, bodies, and sexual desires. Talk about fun on-the-job training! You guys are going to love this job. At times you're going to feel awkward and clumsy. You're probably going to do and say some stupid things, but if you keep in mind that your job is to love this human being, you'll do fine. You will experience each other's rhythms and intricacies in ways you never thought possible."

If the man and woman aren't virgins, I'm still going to challenge them in a similar way: "Aaron, you need to understand that Marissa is not like every woman, and Marissa, Aaron is not like every man. You need to wipe the slate clean, and find out what makes this particular man move, and this particular woman purr."

How does a newlywed couple begin to make music together? It starts by working in tandem to understand what symphony they're trying to play.

THE FIRST PERFORMANCE

"Dr. Leman, you wouldn't believe how beautiful the flowers are going to be. I can't wait for you to see them. And the cake . . . we found this *unbelievably* delicious lemon cake. It just melts in your mouth. Everyone is going to love it. My mom and I must have sampled cake at about a dozen different bakeries! I probably put on five pounds in the process!

"We're still working on the photographer. I've found two who will do, but I'm not sure they're the right ones, so we're still looking. . . ."

When you talk to future brides, you often hear a lot about wedding arrangements. Some brides-to-be can think of nothing else. They'll buy five magazines, each of which weigh about ten pounds, and spend hours looking for just the right dress, the perfect hairdo, and what's in style for the bridesmaids.

But sadly, few spend as much time talking to their future spouse about sexual expectations as they do picking out the flowers for their wedding. Let me tell you something: Three weeks after your wedding, you'll be able to count on one hand the people who can remember what kind of flowers you had at your wedding. But the issue of sexual expectations will shape your household and the satisfaction of your marriage for years to come.

When Sande and I first got married, my expectations were about as high as you can get. I had saved myself for her—and now she was going to get all of me, several times a day! Surprisingly enough, Sande didn't share these same expectations. She thought that we might actually sleep most of the night. Imagine that!

Please, please, *please,* sit down with your future spouse a few weeks before the wedding and get very specific about your expectations, including the first night. So much pain and heartbreak could be spared if couples would simply talk about what they want and don't want. Let's face it: If you can't talk about sex, how intimate is your relationship, really?

Sex: ASAP

When it comes to sex on the honeymoon—or even, frankly, when I'm talking to men in general—I like to talk about sex ASAP. Most people think ASAP means "as soon as possible," but in this case it means sex "as *slow* as possible." The new groom needs to have this slogan burned into his mind if he wants to give his wife a special evening.

For starters, men, walking out of the hotel bathroom, nude and giving a full salute, can be shocking and even horrifying to a woman who has never even seen an erect penis. It's not nearly the turn-on for a woman that some young men apparently think it is. Sadly, this tactic is all too common—you wouldn't believe the number of grooms who try this on the first night. Apparently they're all reading the same book—and it's a bad one!

I tell men to go three times slower and ten times more gently than they think they need to. "You've waited this long," I say, "so another thirty minutes to set the scene won't kill you."

Women, to combat this massive rush, don't be afraid to get very specific with your spouse about your expectations for that first night: "I'd like us to go out to dinner, and then I'd like to take a bath first to relax. When I come out of the bathroom, I'd like you to be wearing some silk shorts and a robe. Let's spend some time kissing, then we can start to undress each other. . . ."

Don't stop there. Particularly if you're virgins (and I truly hope you are), this is not the time or place to try every sexual position and practice known to man and woman. Tell your future husband or wife what you would like to do—and be just as specific about what you think would be going too far on your first night.

This will do two things. One, it will avoid unfortunately common misunderstandings between couples that often get them off to an argumentative start, sexually speaking. And second, it will help the future husband to curb his expectations and get a more realistic view of what the wedding night will be like, avoiding potential disappointment.

For example, though young men are often just as eager to display their own nakedness as they are to see their wife's body, the wife may prefer to come into the bedroom for the first time with subdued lighting or even darkness. She may agree to candlelight but feel a little self-conscious even with that.

To help couples deal with this, I'll give each partner a piece of paper and ask them to write down their expectations for the wedding night. If they write them down ahead of time, they can't change them as they hear their future spouse talking, and it's often a real eye-opener for the future spouses to see how different they are.

This is where we expose the rulebooks that we talked about in chapter two. The guy says, "I just imagine myself waiting for her when she comes out of the bathroom in this beautiful, short, and I mean *really short* nightie, and underneath it she's got this little leopard-skin thong underwear."

"A *thong!*" the young woman cries out.

"Uh, it's still his turn," I gently point out.

"Anyway, I would hold her and caress her and she would kiss me back, and we'd lie down on the bed and . . ."

"You want me to wear *a leopard-skin thong?!*"

Sex ASAP can be likened to those famous Butterball turkeys. I like to tell young men, "Women are a little bit like a Butterball turkey. Butterballs are nice turkeys; they have this thing in the middle that pops up when the turkey is finally ready to be served. Sometimes I wish women had the same thing! But you know what? They operate the same way. You have to do a lot of things before the knob on the turkey pops up. The temperature has to be just right. The timing has to be perfect. The oven needs to be at the right setting.

"Your wife will have a lot of requirements for her to achieve sexual satisfaction as well. You could be satisfied anytime, anywhere. We men can go from frozen to three hundred degrees in about the length of time it takes for a woman to slip out of a nightie. Having difficulty achieving an orgasm is almost never an issue for a young man. But your new bride won't be that way. She needs the right setting. She needs the right temperature."

The groom-to-be usually needs to realize that sex is about far more than genitalia. "You know how you can really turn on your new wife?"

"How?"

He's expecting me to talk about a special caress, a secret position, or something like that. Instead I say, "Look into her eyes before she leaves to take a shower and tell her, 'I'm so thankful that with God's help I was able to save myself for you. I only want to be with you. You're the only one I'll make love to—ever.'"

That will make any young woman who loves the Lord cry. And it will show the young man that sex for a woman involves words and emotions, and other things besides physical groping.

As you discuss the first night, keep your expectations at a realistic level. You have decades to explore each other sexually—the first night will be one (or two, three, or four!) of literally thousands of sexual encounters. It will be special, certainly, but the specialness will come from the meaning of two people coming together as one, not from a particular sexual technique.

To be honest, most people would give their wedding night a C at best, and often that's being charitable. It's a learning experience. Remember, it takes time to make great music.

Important Questions

As your wedding day approaches, you're going to feel closer to your love than ever—and sexual temptation may be at its peak. A very practical way to deal with this is to talk about sex rather than have it. You'll want to be careful about the location, of course—talking in a bedroom can lead to more than verbal play—but stay in public, have a special dessert at a nice restaurant, and go over some of these questions:

1. What are some of the tough issues that surfaced in your dating relationship that you need to talk about? (Is there any unresolved hurt or anger from one partner always trying to push the envelope?)
2. What are some of the fears you have when it comes to marriage? (*Will he still think I look good when I wake up first thing in the morning? What if my breath smells? What if she uses the bathroom after I've just deposited a good bit of last night's dinner and the smell knocks her over?*)

3. What are some of the fears you have about having an active sex life? *(What if she doesn't have an orgasm? What if I don't know how to please him?)*
4. Will you use birth control? If so, what kind?

These will get you started, and you'll no doubt come up with many more on your own. Some couples have a difficult time keeping their pants on just before a wedding because they feel so close to each other. Allow me to let you in on a little secret: talking about issues like the above can be even more intimate than having sex—and you won't feel guilty afterwards. Having sex before a marriage will damage your relationship; Talking about sex will strengthen it. What I've found is that those couples who start having sex the earliest end up talking about it the least—with the result that, later on, they end up being most unsatisfied.

I hope you make the right choice.

Before the First Night

For her

Women, you're going to need a full medical examination at least three months before your wedding. What I'm about to say may be hard for some of you, but I want to give you an assignment: While you're meeting with your doctor, mention your honeymoon and ask her (or him) to specifically examine your genitals. If you are a virgin, your doctor will need to consider your hymen and perhaps your vaginal muscles. If either will make sex painful, your doctor can advise you of preparatory exercises to help prepare your body. Today, there are even graduated vaginal dilators that you can use to gently stretch yourself before the wedding night.

I know this may sound embarrassing, but trust me on this one: It's far better to go through this embarrassment with your doctor than to disappoint yourself and your husband on your honeymoon because sex means nothing but pain to you. With today's medical advancements, there's no reason not to prepare yourself for sexual activity. Your husband's erect penis will be between four and a half to five and a half inches in circumference. That's much bigger than a tampon, and if you aren't preparing your vagina for this activity, you're going to feel more discomfort than pleasure.

One young woman confessed to me that, because she had done nothing to prepare herself for her wedding night, she found the first time to be somewhat painful. When her husband looked at her and noticed that she was wincing, he asked, "What's wrong?" She replied, "Just get it over with."

You don't want that for your first experience, do you?

Think of it this way: You'd never consider entering a marathon without training beforehand, would you? You wouldn't expect to ride a bike for a hundred miles if you had never ridden a bike before; instead, you'd build up your leg muscles and your stamina until you felt confident that you could bike for a hundred miles.

If you're a virgin—or if you've been sexually inactive for a long period of time—your vaginal muscles are going to get a major workout in the near future. You need to get them ready.

In addition to getting your body ready, you'll want to gather a few supplies. I probably don't need to tell you that men love lingerie. Indulge your husband. If your budget allows, pick out several outfits that you can surprise him with throughout the honeymoon.

Secondly, since your body isn't used to sexual activity—or, certainly, not sexual activity this prolonged and frequent—plan on bringing along a vaginal lubricant. You may not need it—and there is no cause for embarrassment if you do—but if you do need it and don't have it, penetration can become difficult and painful for both of you (though saliva is always useful in a pinch). Your husband may feel too embarrassed to buy K-Y jelly or Astroglide, so I usually recommend that the wife do this ahead of time. Of course, if you're using condoms, you shouldn't use Vaseline or a petroleum-jelly-based product since it breaks down the latex.

You also need to prepare yourself mentally and spiritually. Some type of fear is understandable and normal. You don't know what sex is going to be like, and you're about to learn something that is going to be very different from anything you've ever known. In all probability, you won't reach orgasm on your first time, but you will feel warm and close to your husband. If you spend too much time thinking about how you're going to do this or that, you won't do it well.

I like to recommend that couples read through the Song of Songs (or the Song of Solomon, depending on the Bible translation you use). Talk about erotic! It can be very beneficial for religious couples to see how God not only condones, but actively celebrates, married sexuality.

Just relax and remember that sex between a husband and a wife is a very natural thing. As a married couple, there is no place for guilt, and with a committed husband, there is no reason for fear. You're in a safe place, doing a wonderful act that was designed by a very skillful Creator. The penis and vagina are custom fit for each other.

It will mean a lot to your husband if you can talk to him: "Oh, that feels good. I like that." If you have urges or want more of something, tell him. Conversely, if he's being too rough, gently say, "Softer, gentler." Realize that you've got a Brahma bull on your hands and you're like fine china; it may take him a while to learn how to pace himself.

Don't be surprised or angry if your husband climaxes too soon. It's natural for a virgin or a sexually inexperienced male (or even one who hasn't had sex in a long time). Over time your husband will learn to control himself until you have been pleased, but like anything else, ejaculatory control is a skill that needs to be learned. Be gracious; if you make him feel tense about it, it will only get worse in the future.

If you read the section for men, you'll see that I urge them, particularly on the first night, to go slow, to be patient, and to focus on being tender and gentle. I want to give you the opposite advice. The best gift you can give your husband is a sexually enthusiastic mate. Put those inhibitions aside. Do your best to accept your body, and give it without reserve to your husband. Above all, enjoy yourself, and make sure your new husband sees and hears your enjoyment. Help him pleasure you.

For him

First off, if you skipped the "For her" section, please go back and read it. There's much in there that will help you be more sensitive and understanding on your wedding night and throughout the honeymoon. You need to know that most women who are sexually inexperienced will have some soreness when they begin having sex. Your body doesn't work that way, but, to put it bluntly, your body isn't having something repeatedly inserted into it. You can't be too sensitive during the honeymoon; give your wife a break here by going slowly and being a sensitive lover. She may be too sore on day two for an encore performance. Don't take this personally; she may really want to make love, but she may really hurt, too. It's not her fault.

But for the man, here's something that may help. While I don't believe a man needs any prior experience with sexual intercourse before marriage, it will help him in the marriage bed if he learns ejaculatory control before his honeymoon. Since I think premarital sex is unhealthy and immoral, the only way for a man to learn ejaculatory control is through self-stimulation. Just as the woman is preparing her vagina to receive you on your wedding night, you can prepare your body to last longer so you can please her.

Elsewhere in this book we talk about premature ejaculation. Follow the exercises mentioned there, beginning a month or two before the wedding. Keep your thoughts pure; view these more as physical exercises—like push-ups—than anything else. It's most important that you learn how your body reacts, and how to stave off the "point of no return." If you can become familiar with that feeling, you'll be able to back off and learn to control your ejaculation.

You may also consider self-stimulation the morning of, or the night before, your wedding. Again, I know some people will disagree with me here, but physiologically, if a man hasn't ejaculated in a long time, it will be difficult for him not to ejaculate almost immediately upon being stimulated—especially if it's your first sexual experience. Assuming that you want your first time of sexual intercourse with your wife to be memorable *in a positive sense,* the ability to maintain control is a welcome gift.

Don't forget to begin strengthening your pubococcygeus muscles (called PC muscles for short). Use the exercises mentioned elsewhere in this book (page 98–99), as they will assist you in ejaculatory control.

If you choose to use a condom (lubricated would be best) as your form of birth control, you may want to practice putting one on before the wedding night arrives. Your wife, if she is a virgin, won't have any practice with this, nor will she have any way to practice, so for the first night in particular, it's your job to know what to do. And since some wives may prefer reduced lighting or even darkness for the first encounter, you'll be able to spare your wife the embarrassment of having to turn on a light while you try to figure out what goes where.

I hope you're picking up the motivation behind these instructions: Your focus should be on making the first night the most loving, caring experience that your new wife has ever known. You have the ability to shock and disgust her, or tenderly love and please her. This is your only opportunity to create a positive sexual first impression. Be the type of lover who puts his wife first, who thinks about his wife, and who anticipates his wife's needs.

This means that you need to put your wife's emotional needs above your own physical needs. Here's some very practical advice: Don't be surprised—in fact, expect it—if your wife wants to talk about the wedding and relive the entire experience before she shows the slightest interest in getting naked on your wedding night. Young women dream of their weddings; your wife is going to want to revel in it, talk it over, and process the experience by sharing it with you.

You may be wondering what she looks like *inside* that going-away dress, but she's wondering what you thought when the flower girl and the ring bearer bumped into each other; and wasn't it funny when Uncle Albert made that hilarious toast? Oh, and did you see the look on Elaine's face when she saw how big our cake was?

This is part of sex, men. Remember, sex ASAP isn't sex "as soon as possible" but "as slow as possible." Show emotional interest in your wife. Curb your appetites long enough to get emotionally involved with your wife. It is by all accounts sexual foreplay. Treat it as such.

Your wife will probably need and desire ten times the amount of foreplay that you do, especially on the first night. A good idea is to bring some massage oil to help this along. It's relaxing, and a fun way to discover your new wife's body. The touches and warmth and physical closeness will begin heating her up, while you get to enjoy an eyeful (you've waited for it; enjoy it!). But consider carefully what kind of lotion you use; a woman's membranes are very sensitive, so be especially careful around her genitalia. The last thing you want to do is to make her genitals start stinging or burning just when you're getting ready to pay a visit!

If you haven't been intimate with your lover before, one

look at her breasts or naked bottom may be enough to get you turned on immediately. Just climbing onto her naked back and feeling her buttocks against your genitals as you begin a massage can make some inexperienced lovers climax, so take your time, be careful, and try to keep the focus on her. The good news is, if you're young and you do have an "accident" early on, you'll probably be able to get another erection before too long—so don't make that big of a deal about it. Just get a towel, clean up, and keep pleasuring your wife. Mr. Happy will let you know when he's smiling again!

For both of you

Sexually speaking, there are few *worse* ways to start a marriage than with a wedding. Don't get me wrong—you need to get married. But so often, the act of getting married is so exhausting that the couple stumbles into the honeymoon suite well past midnight, with just six hours before they need to wake up to catch an early-morning flight.

Don't do this to yourself. Plan your wedding for *you*. Aunt Millie and Uncle Albert will try to shame you into choosing a day and time that's convenient for them, but you're the ones you should be thinking about.

Choose an early enough hour for the wedding that you won't be out past midnight—unless both of you are night owls and don't really mind that. Try to sleep as much as possible the night before your wedding. Plan your day so you're not exhausted, hungry, and irritable from running yourself ragged.

I know it's tough to eat the day of your wedding, but please try to eat a healthy breakfast and a full lunch. Newlyweds often fail to eat any dinner at all, with the exception of some cake stuffed into their faces at the prompting of an eager photographer.

Both of you will have thought long and hard about this first time. In fact, it's fair to say that you will spend more time thinking about what sex will be like on your wedding night than you will for any other sexual experience in your life. That's only natural—but keep in mind, you're a couple now. You need to think "we," not "me."

This means that whoever is most tired or most conservative is the one who sets the sexual agenda. Your first night, especially, should be a night that both of you cherish and enjoy. It is not the time to demand the fulfillment of endless adolescent fantasies. You've got your entire lives in front of you, so cherish this moment. Season it with tenderness, acceptance, praise, patience, and kindness.

Many counselors (and I am one of them) recommend that newlywed couples take a bath together on their first night. If you allow the wife to enter the water first, she'll feel covered—even though she's naked. The warm water will ease tensions and soothe those sore muscles from standing all day in shoes that are too tight. A lit candle will provide a wonderful ambience—and there's nothing like a clean body to further pique your sexual interest.

Finally, the time is going to come when the two of you are in your hotel room, aroused, excited, and ready to fully consummate your marriage. This is where too many books, unfortunately, stop, leaving couples without the information they want most. What I'm about to share is direct and specific; you don't have to follow it to the letter, of course, but for those of you who want such clear instructions, here goes:

After an extended period of foreplay, the wife should invite her husband to enter her vagina when she's ready. The young husband won't be experienced enough to know when that is, so he should wait for his wife's cue. Besides, telling a man, "I'm ready—please come inside me now" is about the most wonderful and erotic thing a guy could ever hear! (In time, you may discover some even more creative ways to express this!)

Though the penis and vagina are custom-fit, getting them connected isn't always as simple as it sounds, at least not the first time. Gently take hold of your husband's penis and guide his entry into your body. Then rest for a moment; both of you should take a short time-out. The wife needs to allow her muscles to get used to having a penis inside her vagina, and the man could use a breather to avoid immediate ejaculation. Just enjoy the fact that from this moment on, the marriage is fully consummated! Kiss each other softly, and when both of you seem ready, slowly start to move.

Men, you have to be extremely gentle here. "Come inside me" doesn't mean you want to achieve a speed of approximately seventy-five miles an hour, racing down the autobahn to sexual ecstasy. You're driving through a cul-de-sac; you've got to take your time, be careful, and drive gently. First insertion is best done in stages—just the tip of the penis at first; then, if it's comfortable, the wife can signal for her husband to slowly push in further.

Men—don't push all the way in until you're invited to. Your wife may be feeling stretched or even a little pain. Go with her lead. If she is a virgin, the hymen may need to be broken. For some women, this won't be traumatic at all—a momentary twinge of pain that leaves as quickly as it came. A few women may experience a good deal of pain and even bleeding—so much so that they'll need to stop. Prepare yourself, mentally, for this possibility.

Also, don't be surprised if the two of you don't immediately seem to "fit." It takes practice to work out the right angle. Just play around with it and have fun with any miscues. Through trial and error, you'll find the best angle.

If the penis doesn't seem to fit, it may be that the wife's vaginal muscles haven't been sufficiently stretched. Also it could be that her anxiety is unconsciously constricting her muscles. Try to relax. Enjoy this moment; you've waited for it.

Once the husband is inside, he should still look to his wife for his next move. She may want to just lie there and get used to the feeling of having a penis inside her. The husband should not immediately become a battering ram; let your wife direct you.

Do not expect your wife to reach climax simply by your thrusting. Unless you're thrusting in such a way that the clitoris is being directly stimulated, it's not likely that your wife will orgasm. Use your hand to gently caress her clitoris, or, after you have ejaculated and withdrawn, continue stimulating your wife until she has climaxed or until she signals that she is done. Many wives, in fact *most* wives, will not climax the first time they have sex. It may take a while for the two of you to learn how to help the wife reach orgasm. This isn't a "failure" unless you call it such. Your aim is to enjoy each other's bodies. Some couples don't even attempt intercourse on the first night, so don't allow undue expectations to rob the joy of this first and very special time.

Great Expectations

Many couples, after the honeymoon, confess that, in some ways, sex was a bit of a letdown for them. They were told how great sex is supposed to be, and while they enjoyed it, it didn't send them to the moon and back.

There are two things to say about this. First, you'll get better at it, and second, you're right that our society has overblown sex in many ways. The day will come when, given a choice between pork tenderloin and sex, just about every man will eventually, on an occasion or two, actually consider the pork tenderloin.

In some ways, you're probably going to be lousy lovers, but you'll learn like crazy—and can you think of any better on-the-job training? Sex is a wonderful, thrilling experience—but it's only part of your new relationship. An important part, yes, but still only a part.

5

A Very Special Connection

Sexual Positions

Two friends of mine are decidedly on the heavy side. But if you think heavy people have given up on sex, you haven't met my friends.

In fact, one night they decided to get a little adventurous and try one of those "new" sexual positions. They didn't offer to tell me what the position was and I didn't ask, but it must have been a little tricky because midway through the act, both ended up falling off the bed.

Now imagine you're a teenager, quietly reading a book or talking on the phone, when suddenly, at 11 P.M., you hear a good five hundred pounds crashing and banging within the house. You'd check out what was going on, wouldn't you?

Unfortunately, this happened to be the one time my friends forgot to lock their bedroom door. The teenagers, full of alarm, burst right in, and there were Mom and Dad in all their primal glory, meekly trying to untangle themselves while keeping the more sensitive areas of their bodies shielded from public view.

Provided they lock the door first, I think it's a good idea for couples who have been married long enough to have teenagers to still do some experimenting every now and then—but I'm also wary that our culture tries to replace intimacy with technique. In search of the next great sexual experience, some people seem to go out of their way to concoct a ridiculous alignment of bodies or some new method to bring about a new pleasure, when what they really need is to work on their relationship.

People have been having sex for many thousands of years, so any position you find won't be a new one. It might be new to you, but I guarantee you that someone else has tried it.

The truth is, most of us settle down to a few basic positions. Just like most major league pitchers have a favorite pitch, and then two or perhaps three off-speed or curveball or splitter pitches to round out their repertoire, so most married couples settle down into a comfortable routine. Part of this is because we discover what works best for us, given our body shapes and personal preferences. Another part of this is that sometimes a spouse may request something the other spouse wouldn't consider in a million years. "You want me to put *what where?* Not a chance, buddy!"

In fact, while writing this book, I mentioned to my wife one of the positions you're going to read about. Sande was reading a book, wearing a pair of those half-lensed granny glasses, and she simply raised her glance, elevated her eyebrows, and looked at me as if to say, *Don't even think about it.*

Always remember: The best position is no substitute for a healthy relationship. Throughout this book, I'm going to keep coming back to this same truth: Sex is about the quality of your entire love life, not the intricate alignment of your bodies.

MAN ON TOP

This is the classic "missionary" position. The woman is on her back, and the man lies down on top of her. I mention this position first because in most marriages, this is what happens most of the time. It's understandable: Husband and wife are face-to-face, the husband is free to thrust at will, and the alignment doesn't require a gymnast's flexibility. Depending on what shape the man is in, he'll need to be sensitive to use his elbows and take the burden of his body off his wife, but other than that, it's a really good way to make love!

Unfortunately, while this position offers the wonderful benefit of face-to-face contact, it doesn't afford the best stimulation for a woman because it fails to involve the clitoris, unless you make a few adjustments. However, many of the adjustments require a somewhat limber wife.

Try putting one or two pillows underneath your wife's lower back. Your aim is to get her pelvis to tilt upwards so that it comes in contact with the husband's body as he penetrates her. Another way to do this (though this is the one that requires a certain degree of flexibility) is to have the woman either put her feet on the man's shoulders or wrap her legs around his neck. Since every body is different, you'll need to make minor adjustments until you hit the right spot, but if you hit it, believe me, the wife will know it—and she won't let you stop.

The man can help as well. Instead of seeing this position as an "in and out" enterprise, he should consider it "rock and roll." If the woman tilts her pelvis up while the man performs a downstroke, creating more of a rocking effect, the clitoris can become very stimulated.

If you can make this position work, it's a good "hands free" route to orgasm for the wife.

Variations:

1. The woman can lift her knees, allowing for deeper penetration.
2. The wife can put her legs over her husband's shoulders.
3. The wife can wrap her legs around her husband's torso, drawing him closer.
4. The husband can also experiment where he puts his legs for a different sensation. At times, he may put one leg outside his wife's leg, with the other inside her legs; or, put both his legs outside his wife's legs. Every variation creates a different sensation, so feel free to experiment.
5. Instead of the man lying on top of his wife, he can kneel between her legs while she lies back, draping her thighs over his legs. The husband keeps his back straight (so his body is perpendicular to hers), and can work on finding the right angle to stimulate his wife's clitoris.
6. While the husband is on top, the wife can grab her husband's hip bones (or buttocks, if you prefer), and rock his hips to and fro. In general, a man likes it when the woman takes initiative to get what she wants, and the sensation of being pulled in deeper is a very nice corollary. For the woman, you gently take control of the speed, direction, timing, and depth of his thrusts. Both of you win with this move!

WOMAN ON TOP

I love this one, as I think most men do. What's so nice about having the wife be on top, for a man at least, is that the husband gets a wonderful view. And since eyes are such an important part of a man's lovemaking, this one tops it off. What's nice about this for a woman is that she can control a lot of things from up top. She determines the speed and angle of thrusting, as well as the depth of the thrusting. This position also encourages the woman to be more aggressive.

Because the woman is "on view," this position requires a confident wife who isn't too self-conscious about her body; otherwise she'll feel like she's on display. But for those wives who enjoy this, it can be a real treat for the husband since he gets an eyeful. Also advantageous is the fact that both of the man's hands are completely free, providing many pleasurable options. If he has a bad back or painful knees (as many men do), this may be the easiest and most comfortable way for him to make love.

Another benefit of this position is that it assumes the wife is enthusiastically taking part—men like that more than anything else. A wife who is enjoying sex and visibly getting into it is one of the most thrilling experiences any husband could have.

To bring the clitoris more into play in this position, think angles. The wife can either lean back—perhaps using her husband's knees as support (if he raises them up), or lean forward. If you work these angles, you'll eventually find the exact place where the wife finally goes, "Oh, yeah . . ." and then you're on your way.

Not only are the man's hands free in this position, but so are the woman's. Particularly if she's leaning back, the wife can put one hand behind her and gently caress her husband's testicles or perineum (that oh-so-sensitive stretch of skin between a husband's testicles and his anus).

Variations:
1. The woman can face away from the husband, looking at his feet. Trust me, wives—some of the men will really like this view, even though it may make you feel conspicuous.
2. The wife can lean over so she's not sitting up, providing many of the benefits of this position without making her feel like she's "on display."

3. The husband can lift his knees, providing his wife with something to lean against.
4. The wife, if she lies prone, can use her husband's shins or feet as "push off" points to gain leverage in her forward thrusting.

SIDE BY SIDE

After thirty-five years of marriage and active lovemaking, I think I know what I'm talking about when I say that the most intimate and erotic act between a husband and a wife is kissing. Two lovers can participate in this most sensuous act for a long time. In fact, I know of one young couple who, before they were married, spent *seven hours* kissing on a boat on a leisurely Saturday afternoon. They never got into petting or anything deeper—they just enjoyed a workday's worth of kissing!

Most married couples will never experience this because after one or two *minutes* of kissing, hubby is all too eager to insert tab A into slot B. The side-by-side position can bring married lovers back to this wonderful building block of physical intimacy, because there's nothing nicer than a sweet, passionate kiss.

There are two ways to go side by side, of course. The way that encourages kissing is to be face-to-face. The other position is when the husband enters from behind the wife. This is often called "spooning."

Spooning generally offers the gentlest form of intercourse, and it is frequently prescribed for pregnancy, illness, or just plain weariness. It's not the best position for men for whom penis length is an issue, however.

Variations:
1. If the husband lifts his upper leg and bends it at the knee, the wife can drape her upper leg over her husband's body while inserting her lower leg between her husband's two

legs. This puts the penis right where it needs to be in relation to the vagina!

2. A "scissors" variation isn't really side by side, but it's close: The husband lies on his side, while the wife lies on her back. She lifts the leg closest to her husband up in the air, and the husband places his upper leg between his wife's two legs. His lower leg is under her bottom. While this isn't the best position for active thrusting, it allows the husband to use his hand to stimulate the clitoris, or to use his penis to rub against her clitoris. He can also slip his penis inside her vagina. This can be a very pleasurable variation during a pregnancy, when the wife's stomach is large and protruding.

SITTING

I like any position, but there's something nice about a woman sitting on a man: on a chair, on a bed, on a desk—or in some secluded hideaway, sitting in the outdoors on a rock.

Sitting is often an "on the way" position rather than the final one. That is, a couple will often start out making love in this position, and then move to another one that provides for more vigorous thrusting before each partner reaches climax.

One of the nice things about this position is that you can use it to flirt a little bit. For example, the husband can use just the tip of his penis to massage his wife's clitoris, or the wife can teasingly take the husband's penis in her hand and just barely put it into her vagina, then take it out, then partway put it back in.

Another wonderful thing about making love this way is that both partners have full access to each other and both partners also have both arms free. Since you're facing each other, this is a very emotionally intimate position. Both of you have your hands free to caress each other's face, rub each other's neck, or even provide a gentle back rub.

This can take us back to the importance of kissing; if you're sitting facing each other, you're lined up perfectly for all sorts of pleasurable play.

Since this tends to be a slower form of sexual expression, it's probably not for those nights when the two of you just want to "do it." It's better for the "let's warm up slowly and take our time" kind of nights.

Variations:

1. Instead of the wife sitting on her husband, she and he can sit facing each other with firm pillows behind them. With each partner leaning back (sort of like you would on the edge of a swimming pool) keep moving toward each other until your genitals connect. Don't make this more complicated than it is; just let your legs go wherever they're most comfortable.
2. The wife can sit on her husband, facing *away* from him. She can then determine the speed and depth of thrusting.
3. This is a good position to take "on the road." Since love-making in the great outdoors can lead to certain logistical problems (creepy crawlies, rocks and sticks poking you in the back), the sitting position allows the husband to bear the brunt of this discomfort while the wife gets a nice soft seat. It also allows you to make love by just dropping your pants rather than taking them all the way off (but hopefully you'll find a place where there's no chance of being discovered).

MAN KNEELING BEHIND THE WOMAN

This one gets talked about a good bit in the counseling room, for this reason: It's a position that most every man would like to try, but at the same time, it sometimes makes women feel a little uncomfortable. From a psychologist's point of view, the reason men like it so much is that there is something in a man's psyche that makes it very erotic for him to enter a woman from behind. It's probably one of the more animalistic urges that men get from time to time, and let's be honest: Sometimes there is an "animalistic" urge behind sex.

Men, the reason some women feel uncomfortable with this is that they may fear you'll be turned off looking right at their bottom—you could be thrilled with the view, but your wife may have a hard time believing that. Women also tend to be less than excited about this position because they can't see you at all. You've got a full, uninhibited view (and the sensuousness of a woman's back gets far too little attention in our culture, so obsessed are we with breasts), but your wife is looking at the bedroom wall. Since sex is such an emotional experience for a woman, this may be one of the least satisfying, emotionally speaking, of all the positions.

Now that you understand each other a little better, perhaps you can still use this for when a "quickie" is in order, or when a wife wants to give her husband a special treat. There are times when a guy wakes up hornier than a toad but the couple needs to get out of bed in just ten or fifteen minutes. A loving wife might say, "Honey, I don't have time for a long love-making session—although there's nothing I'd like more—but I'll tell you what. You've got ten minutes; name your position."

"I see myself as a shortstop."

"Not that kind of position, dummy!"

"But I've got a strong right arm . . ."

"Oh yeah, well, let's see what else you can use. . . ."

In this instance, the wife may be willing to accommodate for a position she normally wouldn't choose, because let's face it: She's having sex to please her husband more than anything else. If some of you wives are surprised at the thought of a woman doing this for her husband, I hope you're beginning to see how much you can love your man by sending him to work with this need met rather than having him leave the house trying to keep his lustful thoughts at bay. You can turn down a husband and forget about sex for ten hours, but remember this: Your rejected husband won't forget about it just because you do.

THE ART OF MAKING LOVE

Some books will go into more wild and exotic positions, but I'm guessing that not too many wives have either the size or flexibility of Olga Korbut and Mary Lou Retton. The positions we've mentioned account for well over 90 percent of a couple's lovemaking. If you think you've invented some other position, feel free to send the description to me and I'll run it by my wife (but just between you and me, I don't think it's gonna fly).

When you talk about positions, you're talking about science—aligning this body part with that body part—and frankly, I prefer to think of lovemaking as an art. It's what you do with the position, not the position itself, that results in satisfying sex.

To heat things up a bit—to flirt with fun—try using your body parts creatively while you're in one of the positions. For example, use a toe instead of a hand, or put your tongue somewhere besides your partner's mouth. You can imagine how quickly things can move from there.

Use positions to set the mood or accommodate a particular desire. For example, if you're tired, or somebody isn't feeling well, that person should be on the bottom, allowing the person on top to do most of the work. It's only fair.

If the wife is concerned about her husband's generous size, occasionally even being hurt by the girth of his penis, her best position is normally going to be on top, where she can control the depth and speed of penetration. (In such circumstances, you might also try "spooning," which is what a lot of pregnant women do when they lose mobility and still want to accommodate their husband.) For these couples, your worst position is probably going to be the husband entering from behind. If hubby gets carried away, he might not even see that his wife is hurting. If your large husband particularly enjoys this position, you'll need to be up-front about your concerns and remind him to be gentle.

As you set the mood and tone of your lovemaking session, you'll soon learn that certain positions tend to accentuate certain emotions. If you want to relax, try a position where everything matches up—your face with her face, your hands with her hands, your legs with her legs. Take it slow, and enjoy the power of lining up together.

If you're in that animalistic state where you just want to "do" each other, having the husband behind might be a thrill. If you want to work up to something, try the sitting position (or even standing!). If the wife is feeling frisky, she may enjoy climbing on top of her man and being in control.

Above all, have freedom within your "coupledom" to do what you want to do. All this goes back earlier to when I talked about a husband reading his wife's "winds." For most of us guys, we don't care where or when or how a wife wants to have sex; if she's willing, we are! (One man I interviewed told me, "for a man, even bad sex is good sex!") But for many women, the whole "aura" of the experience has to be laid out. Depending on her mood, one, two, or three positions might be offensive; others might be absolute dead ends, killing all desire right away.

Also remember, wives, that being accommodating about any particular position is only part of the art of lovemaking. What you do in that position verbally will matter more than what position you're in. Your husband would probably rather do the missionary position one hundred times out of a hundred if you're howling and groaning and moaning, as compared to doing the most athletic positions imaginable if you're saying, "Hurry up and get it over with" or even worse than that, "Pull my nightie down when you're through."

I like to encourage wives to be "cheerleaders" when they make love. I'm not talking about some adolescent fantasy where you actually dress up in a cheerleader's outfit and bring pom-poms to bed (although, now that you mention it . . .). What I'm talking about is how you encourage your man during the process of making love.

What drives a man most is when a woman speaks words or acts in such a way that shows she is really into this: Digging her nails into his back, asking him to give her more, or saying things like, "I want you in me deeper," sticking her tongue in his ear, or panting like a puppy dog—whatever it is you do to let your husband know you're into it, do it!

If your husband knows you're heating up, in most cases he'll want to help you finish. Scratch that: He'll go out of his way to get you there. He'll dig down a little deeper; he'll gather the last reserves of strength. He wants to hear that orgasm ripping through your body!

6

The Big "O"

$\mathcal{M}$any women are surprised when I tell them that a large percentage of men are jealous of their orgasms. Though women often initially have more difficulty than men achieving an orgasm (particularly for the first time), once they do—well, from a guy's perspective, it looks like the world is exploding.

Consider that famous scene from the movie *When Harry Met Sally,* when Meg Ryan fakes an orgasm in the New York deli, to everyone's delight (especially the lady who candidly says, "I'll have what she's having"). If you were walking by a room and heard what was going on, you might be tempted to call the police!

Don't get me wrong: We men love our climaxes. Those intense few seconds are well worth the effort it took to get there. But when we watch our wives, we see them build slowly and then ride seemingly wave after wave of pleasure. Even more, when they finally reach orgasm, they can keep going! Most of us men—at least those of us over thirty—are down and out for at least half an hour (if not a day or two). But women have the physiological ability to be like the Energizer Bunny: They keep going and going and going. . . .

Physiologically, the only thing limiting a woman's potential number of orgasms in any given sexual encounter is the woman herself. Some women simply feel that one is enough. Others grow weary and lack the stamina to pursue something so intense. But a woman's body can keep going in a way that a man's just can't.

Among women, multiple orgasms vary. Some women seem to ride a wave of orgasms, with one following after the other in a phenomenon often called "extended sexual orgasms." Other women come to orgasm and then go through a refractory or resting period before they feel ready to orgasm again.

Women also have more control over their orgasms. While men can control their ejaculations before they reach a certain point, physiologically, a man will eventually cross a line where he simply can't control whether the orgasm is going to occur or not (which is why men need to learn what it feels like *before* they reach this point of no return). Once men reach a certain point, the orgasm is going to happen.

Women, on the other hand, can stop at virtually any point. A wife can be riding the waves of ecstasy, just seconds away from falling into the ocean of orgasm, but then hear a baby cry or think she hears a neighbor outside the window, and suddenly, she's as far from an orgasm as Australia is from the North Pole. (My wife Sande personally subscribes to the half-mile rule. She's mentally ready for sex as long as no one is within a half-mile of the bed upon which that sex will occur.)

Another difference between a man's and woman's orgasm is based on previous sexual experience. Let's say a husband has been away for two weeks on an extended business trip. A woman's body can go into a sort of slow-burning hibernation when she is not sexually active. If it has been a while since her last sexual experience, she'll frequently need more time, not less, to heat up.

A man, on the other hand, is just the opposite. If he hasn't had sex for two weeks, he may be riding a hair trigger, the famed "thirty-second wonder." His body is going to be revving a hundred miles an hour *before his wife even touches him.* Just the *thought* of coming home might be enough to cause an erection, whereas the wife will likely need to be "reawakened" and brought along a little more slowly. If the man hasn't reached orgasm in a long period of time, it will be more difficult for him to maintain ejaculatory control. He likely won't need any foreplay, while his wife, on the other hand, will need extended foreplay.

The potential conflicts are obvious!

GETTING THERE

I probably have a somewhat biased view, since most people who come to see me by definition have problems serious enough to warrant paying someone to talk about them. But with this biased view, I've found that one of the most common sexual problems in marriage is women having difficulty achieving orgasms.

The most common case is one I talked about with Jessica and Darren. Jessica confessed that, even after ten years of marriage, achieving an orgasm was difficult. "I've had some baby ones," she said, "but that's about it."

What I tried to get that couple to see is how important a vigorous female orgasm is to both partners. "Jessica," I said, "the first thing you need to understand is that by the way God designed you, you have the capability to have an orgasm that will make Darren's jaw drop to the floor. You'll be like an uncaged tiger, and you need to work toward that."

Some women expect an orgasm to come out of thin air, without any work on their part—but it doesn't happen that way for most women. Men are just the opposite. I doubt there's a man alive who hasn't reached orgasm at least once in his life. Even if he's celibate and a virgin, he's had a nocturnal emission (or twelve). Furthermore, it's not difficult to tell whether a man has reached orgasm. The physical symptoms—ejaculation being the primary one—are rather obvious.

In most marriages, the man's main concern with reaching orgasm is putting it off until the wife is satisfied. Reaching orgasm isn't normally the problem; prolonging it is.

Many women, on the other hand, have never reached orgasm. Other women aren't sure if they have. The intensity and quality of orgasm varies from woman to woman, and many times, it's difficult to tell.

The best way for a woman to know whether she has reached an orgasm is if she feels frustrated and "pent up" after sex, or relaxed and satisfied. An orgasm brings a point of release, where built-up tension explodes and then dissipates. One writer has called it a "pelvic sneeze."[9] I think that's a great description, because all of us have experienced the buildup to a good sneeze—your whole body seems to scrunch up until, finally, you sneeze and feel the relief. That's what an orgasm is like. Sexual caressing builds up pleasure, but it also creates a sensitive tension that demands to be fulfilled.

If you're having difficulty achieving an orgasm, here are a few suggestions.

1. Have the right goal.

Allow me to be blunt: If the whole goal of your sexual activity is to have an orgasm, you're going down the wrong track. There are many different degrees of pleasure in sex. For some

[9]Clifford and Joyce Penner, *Getting Your Sex Life Off to a Great Start: A Guide for Engaged and Newlywed Couples* (Dallas: Word Publishing, 1994), 109.

of us, scratch my back and I'm a happy guy; give me a foot rub with lotion and I'm satisfied. If you become too narrow—having to have an orgasm or, even more narrow, having to have an orgasm at the exact same time as your spouse—it only makes things worse.

The goal of sexuality is to express oneness and intimacy with your mate. It's a loving response toward someone to whom you are committed for life. For those of us with children or those who want children, it's a way to build a family.

Sex is so profound and meaningful and deep on so many levels that we cheapen it when we reduce it to, "Well, did you have an orgasm or not?" Such language belongs in the Playboy mansion, not a marital bedroom.

Even once a woman has learned to have orgasms, she probably won't have one every time she has sex. Very few women experience orgasm with every sexual encounter. If you do, you're a very fortunate woman, but you're also in the small minority. Sometimes a woman will simply pleasure her husband (other times a husband may pleasure his wife without his having an orgasm). Marital sex presents all sorts of situations where orgasm isn't possible or where it's passed over for any number of reasons.

2. Having an orgasm is a learned skill.

I might as well keep being blunt—what I find is that a lot of women are lazy when it comes to this area of their life. They assume it's their husband's responsibility to give them an orgasm, or they think an orgasm will just mystically appear some night under the covers. Sorry, honey—unless you're very lucky, that isn't going to happen. For a very small percentage of women, orgasms come without much work. For most women, it takes a bit of experience to regularly orgasm. For another few, it takes a lot of hard work and discovery.

Think of it this way: If you knit, were you able to create an

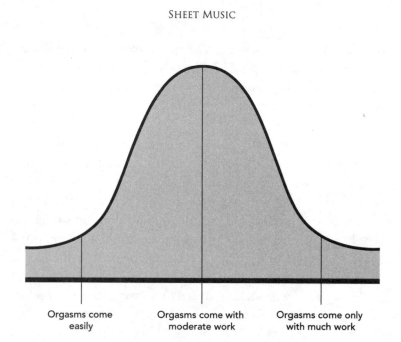

| Orgasms come easily | Orgasms come with moderate work | Orgasms come only with much work |

intricate design the first time you picked up a knitting needle? Certainly not! If you golf, were you able to drive the ball over two hundred yards the first time you picked up a driver? I bet you weren't!

Why should sex be any different? It takes time, experience, knowledge, and practice to excel at being a good lover.

Number one, if you're having trouble achieving an orgasm, don't do what a lot of the women's magazines suggest: Don't imagine another or a former lover; don't use pornography or X-rated films or anything that would cheapen your relationship and sense of intimacy with your husband.

Instead, get to know yourself well enough that you can help your husband learn what makes you heat up. Even if your husband had sexual experience before marriage, your body is unique and requires a unique approach. Help him find this path.

In other words, you've got some exploring to do—you've got to learn what makes you tick.

3. Become more aware of your own personal sexual response.
Take a long, hot bath. Put out some candles, pamper yourself, and then, yes, start touching yourself. Find out what feels good. Don't make orgasm a goal here, but do notice what awakens pleasure and desire. Don't be afraid to explore your genitals. Find out how your clitoris likes to be rubbed. Some women need to be very indirect in their touch, caressing the labial lips or approaching the clitoris from above instead of directly on it; others prefer direct contact once their arousal reaches a certain level.[10]

You may have to do this several times before you begin to discover your body's path to sexual pleasure. Take the time, and give yourself plenty of leeway. This isn't a race, and nobody is holding a calendar above your bed.

Some of my readers might be getting red in the face right now, thinking, *Dr. Leman, are you asking me to masturbate?*

Sometimes I hate that word, simply because of the connotations that have become associated with it. When husbands or wives stimulate themselves to climax to avoid intimacy with their spouse or to participate in pornography or something like that, they are, in my view, acting in a selfish and destructive manner. However, when a wife is learning to respond sexually to her husband so that the two of them can enjoy a deeper and richer sexual experience, she is working toward greater intimacy, not less—just like a husband who is trying to learn ejaculatory control or who is on a long business trip may occasionally use self-stimulation to strengthen his marriage rather than weaken it.

So yes—there are times when masturbation is wrong and addictive and should be avoided. There are other times when getting familiar with your body is an unselfish act as you train

[10]See Chapter 8 for more information.

yourself to become a better lover for your spouse. You know if what you are doing is selfish and running away from your spouse, or if what you are doing is preparing you to draw closer to your spouse.

So many women had mothers refer to vaginas as "down there," as if they didn't have one, or as if they just had a giant, unmentionable hole. If you're coming into marriage with that kind of baggage, of course you're going to feel uncomfortable about sexual touch. But think of it this way: It's not sinful to touch your ankle if you're concerned that you may have sprained it; it's not wrong to enjoy the pleasurable sensation of brushing your hair. If you can touch every other part of your body, why not touch the most sensitive parts?

When a woman gets ready to have a baby she usually practices her breathing so that when the event comes she's able to meet the challenge. Why should sex be any different? You're learning how to prepare for sex by learning to have a climax.

So yes, let your fingers go walking through the yellow pages! Tell yourself that this is good and right. Your Creator designed you to give and to receive sexual pleasure; the shame is in settling for something less than that. You want to be a good lover to your husband and the best way to be a good lover is to learn to really enjoy sex, which means learning how to have an orgasm. That's a wonderful gift, the best gift you can give a man, so no matter how long you have to shop and search to bring it home, do so!

Another option is to ask your spouse to experiment with you in a "nonintercourse" touching session. He can let his fingers do the walking, and both of you can try out what pleases you.

4. Practice Kegel exercises.
What have become known as "Kegel exercises" (after Dr. Arnold Kegel) are helpful for both men and women as enhancers

of sexual lovemaking. The exercises are designed to help women become more orgasmic, and to help men delay their orgasm.

Kegel exercises work the pubococcygeus muscles (PC, for short), the same muscles that stop the flow of urine. The first thing you need to do is to locate your PC muscles. The easiest way to do this is to gently place one finger in your vagina and try to "squeeze" your finger. Those muscles that you contract are the PC muscles. (If you prefer not to discover your PC muscles in this fashion, take this approach—while sitting on the toilet, try stopping your urine midstream.)

Well-developed PC muscles are helpful for a number of reasons. Not only do they have the added benefit of helping to decrease incontinence, but they can add a lot to your sex life as well. For women, these muscles can be used to contract around the penis, giving your husband a tighter feel. These contractions become sort of like a penile massage, a nice treat for your man. They will also aid you as part of your journey to become more orgasmic.

Once you've located the muscles, start contracting them and holding them for just a few seconds, ten times to begin with, working your way up from there. Once you become more used to performing these contractions, you can do them while you carpool, while you're on the phone, or any time, without anyone knowing. It might be helpful for you to get into a routine, just so you can remember to do them—like during a regular evening commute, or a morning television program.

5. Accept responsibility.
Too many women don't accept responsibility for their own orgasms. They need to be an active participant, not just a receiver of their husband's advances. If you want to frustrate a man, tell him nothing. Make him keep throwing darts into the dark, hoping he gets lucky.

Without in any way sounding condemning or accusatory, talk to your husband as much as you can, being encouraging in the process. Tell him what feels good. If you think he's getting close, but still missing it, gently take his hand and say, "Right there, oh yes, honey, you've got it now. . . ." Who knows how many great symphonies are created with the husband's index finger? But here's the challenge: Every woman is different, so help your husband find your favorite spots.

6. Remember that sex is about relationship more than technique. If you're having difficulty responding sexually, the problem may not be whether you're touched in the right place, or whether your husband has the necessary lovemaking skills, or anything else that takes place under the covers. It might be that you're dealing with some unsettled issues—maybe past sexual abuse, maybe a recent hurtful conversation, forty-eight hours before, that keeps you from opening yourself up to your husband for pleasure.

Don't assume that the conversation was with your spouse. Maybe you got ticked off at your mother-in-law; maybe someone criticized your parenting skills or did something else that is making you feel inadequate. You're a whole, complete, and complex person. Sex sometimes brings out the raw nature in us, and hurts can manifest themselves by how we respond sexually.

It may be that your bedroom isn't a safe enough environment for you; maybe you're worried that the kids will come in or hear your response. Perhaps just hearing a toilet flush is enough to stop you cold.

If this is the case, think about getting away for a while. Splurge on a hotel room where no one you care about can possibly hear or see what's going on, and where you know no one will walk through the door.

In other words, look at your relationship holistically. Your marriage is about much more than whether you're achieving orgasms.

This points out a major difference between men and women. Many men think of sex as the great eraser. To them, if the car is broken down, all they need to do is have sex and everything will feel better (even if the car still isn't running). Get in a fight with your wife? Have sex and everything will be okay (even if you never talk about the issues). Men generally don't need to talk through the fact that their wife is angry at them because they didn't cut the lawn. To the male mind, "since we had sex, everything must be okay."

A woman doesn't work that way. For her, problems erase sex; sex doesn't erase problems. If a wife is upset at her husband, she may shut down sexually: "What do you mean the problem is solved? We haven't even talked about it yet!" If she's worried that there won't be enough money to pay the mortgage in three days, she may lose all sexual desire.

If you're having difficulty achieving orgasm, look at the entire relationship, and then look at your whole life. Are other issues keeping you distracted?

7. Men, be supportive.

Men: For the most part, slow, easy, and soft is the key. (Of course, there comes a point when your wife won't be interested in soft. Suddenly she's Jane the Barbarian, and she wants all the steam that Tarzan can muster!) But, in general, you need to create a relaxing environment for your wife by not focusing too heavily on orgasm: "Was that it, honey? Did you have one?" Hey, buddy, if you have to ask, she didn't have one! Help her feel good, but don't pressure her.

It will also help if your wife knows you're enjoying the process. If she thinks you're bored or impatient, she may shut down. If you act bored and impatient, quite frankly, you're being cruel. I've seen men spend hours trying to get a car engine to purr like a kitten, yet seemingly resent that their wife needs thirty or forty minutes of foreplay to adequately heat up. Your attitude should be, *whatever it takes.*

Besides, it's to your benefit to help your wife enjoy herself sexually. I've said this before and I'll say it again: The best part of sex for me is knowing I'm giving pleasure to my wife. Sometimes I think I enjoy her orgasms even more than she does! Putting in the time and effort to help your wife get there is well worth it.

You're going to have to become familiar with your wife's love language to know what will help her respond sexually. If words of affirmation get her going, say sweet but provocative phrases: "Honey, you're so amazingly sexy. You're so wet. I can't believe your body!" Some women may not like that kind of talk; others will eat it up. You've got to know your wife, and that means becoming more communicative.

Now that we've talked about helping women speed up, let's talk about helping men slow down.

DELAYING ORGASM (PREMATURE EJACULATION)

One time, early in our marriage, Sande had me about as excited as I've ever been. She looked too good to be true, and I remember thinking, *What did I ever do to deserve this beautiful woman?* The fact that she was excited, that she wanted *me,* was about the biggest turn-on I could imagine. I was ready to give her my love all night long. I planned for us to engage in hours of pleasurable play, riding the heights of ecstasy until the dawn light forced us to stop.

And so began the most intense thirty seconds of my life.

Okay, maybe it was 120 seconds, but I still stopped a couple hours short of midnight, much to my dismay.

It happens to just about every man eventually. Ejaculating

before you want to is one of the more common problems amongst men (that and impotence).

It's important for women to understand this (so men, if your wife skipped this section and handed the book off to you, hand it back to her!). A basic ignorance about the physiology of male and female arousal and orgasm can lead to a lot of accusations. Because women can control their orgasms, and because they can stop at virtually any point in the process, they sometimes assume the same is true for a man. When a woman tells her husband to wait, and he tries, but the anxiety produces the exact opposite response, well, sometimes she takes it personally, as if the husband was purposely being selfish.

In certain cases, I suppose some men are being selfish—but most often, premature ejaculation has more to do with lacking the ability to control ejaculation than it does with selfishness. Once a man reaches the "point of no return," orgasm will happen within seconds—and there's nothing he can do to stop it.

Just about every man runs up against this problem at one time or another. Particularly if he hasn't had sex in a while, ejaculatory control may be difficult for a man to maintain. But a persistent and consistent inability to control orgasm (meaning, you can't choose when you allow yourself to orgasm, and more frequently than not you reach orgasm before you want to) is a problem that, in most cases, can be cured.

Just what is premature orgasm? Masters and Johnson discovered that the average male will ejaculate after two minutes of vigorous thrusting. Most men can delay this by changing the pace and depth of their thrusts, but if you're going all out and end up ejaculating within about two minutes, that's not premature, that's average. The problem is that very few women will be sufficiently stimulated after 120 seconds of thrusting! (Which is another good argument for helping women reach orgasm during foreplay; the vast majority of women reach orgasm through stimulation of the clitoris, not thrusting.)

I think the best indicator of premature orgasm is this: Are you able to choose when you want to orgasm, or do you, more often than not, end up climaxing before you want to? If you habitually reach climax within seconds of entering your wife, you're prone to premature ejaculation.

Women, please be sensitive here. I know you can't even imagine screaming and hollering and collapsing into an orgasm as soon as your husband first enters your body, but it's not all that uncommon for a male to sometimes ejaculate as soon as penetration occurs. Just like a man has to be patient with a woman who seemingly takes forever to reach orgasm, so a woman needs to be patient with a man who comes too early.

Therapists have developed three methods of learning to increase ejaculatory control (and not a single one of them is pleasurable!). If we took a vote of males across the country, this is one section guys might wish we just took out. Some men have the attitude, unfortunately, that says, *So, I blew it. You made me so frisky, I couldn't stop! What's the big deal?*

It's *not* a big deal if it happens once in a while. It *becomes* a big deal if it happens more often than not.

Men with this lackadaisical attitude are being just as selfish as women who do nothing to help themselves become more orgasmic. Don't use your marriage and your wife's commitment as an excuse to become a lazy lover; use it as motivation to become an expert in bed.

As a precursor to the following therapies, start exercising your PC muscles with the Kegel exercises. To find the PC muscles, clench whatever you clench if you want to stop urinating midstream. Those are the ones you want to work on, and doing so will improve ejaculatory control.

Two or three times a day, contract the PC muscles ten to twenty times. Don't use your abdominal muscles—the most common mistake when doing this exercise—instead, make sure you're contracting the pelvic muscles. Every few contractions, throw in a long hold, for about three seconds.

These exercises are simple, and they can be done in the car, while watching television, or sitting at your desk—and no one will notice. The time requirement is also minimal—less than five minutes a day. Keep in mind that you may need to do these exercises for two weeks or even longer before you notice much change.

1. Stop-start.

The first method of working on premature ejaculation is called the *stop-start* method. There are any number of descriptions out there on it, but the most thorough step-by-step method is contained in Dr. Bernie Zilbergeld's book *The New Male Sexuality*. While I don't agree with all that Dr. Zilbergeld teaches regarding sexuality, his work on this method is pretty exhaustive and easy to follow. What I'm giving you is a greatly abbreviated form; if this shorter version doesn't work for you, you may want to consult Dr. Zilbergeld's book.

The husband begins the stop-start method by knowing he is going to go through several stages. He'll begin several practices on his own and work up to actual love play with his wife. The goal is to achieve fifteen minutes of stimulation without ejaculation.

Beginning by himself, a husband should stimulate himself until he is aroused, focusing on becoming increasingly aware of his body's mechanics. Do not use pornography or inappropriate fantasies during this time; filling your mind with such pollutants will only harm your marriage. Your goal is to become a better lover for your wife.

Every man has a "point of no return," when the muscles surrounding your penis start moving and ejaculation is certain. You want to stimulate yourself but stop short of the point of no return. As soon as you feel yourself getting too close, stop all stimulation and wait for the feeling to subside. Then start back up again.

Younger men may need to pause longer than older men, but again, your goal is to receive fifteen minutes of stimulation without needing to ejaculate. If you fail to stop in time, just chalk that one up to experience and try again a day or two later.

These exercises can be performed three times a week. Once you've achieved a certain amount of control—that is, when you can withstand near constant (but varied in intensity) stimulation for at least fifteen minutes—then you can begin engaging in "start-stop" love play with your wife. You'll need her understanding and cooperation.

Once you are aroused and your wife is ready, enter your wife slowly, but have her lie still. Wait until you feel comfortable inside the vagina and don't feel the need to climax. Then slowly begin to move in and out. If you feel the need to ejaculate, stop all motion. This may not be a pleasurable experience for your wife—she's going to have to be a willing and docile partner, looking forward to the time when you have gained better control (and she'll benefit immensely). This is actually "practice" more than it is actual intercourse.

Once again you want to remain in your wife's vagina for fifteen minutes without ejaculating. It may take you several times until you last this long, but work at it. Over time, you'll gain a better understanding of what brings you immediately to climax, as well as how to vary your thrusts and contain your motions so you can last as long as you want.

The two following methods can be used in conjunction with the stop-start method.

2. The squeeze technique.

The second exercise is the *squeeze* technique, which can be used in conjunction with the stop-start method. When the husband senses ejaculation may be coming soon, he pulls his penis out of his wife's vagina, and she grasps his penis with her thumb and index and middle fingers. Her thumb should be on the underside of the shaft, and her two fingers should be just below the hood of the penis (if it's more comfortable for her to have her thumb on the upper side and her fingers on the lower side, that's okay too). She should then gently but firmly (and steadily) squeeze for several seconds. In most instances, this will stop the man from progressing to the point of ejaculatory inevitability. The couple can then begin having intercourse again and repeat the squeeze as needed.

Where this method fails is usually when the man waits too long to ask his wife to apply the squeeze technique. It all goes back to the man learning to understand his body and sexual responses.

3. The scrotal pull.

There are varying reports as to the success of this method, but it's easier to apply than the squeeze technique, and some couples have found it to be just as successful. When the husband senses an orgasm may be building (but before he gets to ejaculatory inevitability), he should ask his wife to intervene. She reaches out and gently (*very* gently) takes his scrotum into her hand. Without squeezing his testicles (which would be painful), she pulls the scrotum down, away from his body, and holds it there for a few seconds. Once the man's excitement has subsided, the couple can begin engaging in intercourse again.

MAKING THE EFFORT

Experiment and find out which method (or methods) works best for you—but remember: There's no reason to settle for second best. Women can learn to have orgasms, and men can learn to delay theirs. It may take a little work, but the rate of success is very high.

Because men are prone to premature ejaculation, I like to tell them that the penis is the last thing they should use to make love with. Why make love with your penis when there are so many other things to use?

"What do you mean, Dr. Leman?"

Well, there are your lips, your tongue, your feet, your hands, your fingers, your knee and elbow, your breath, your teeth—and many other parts if you'll just get a little creative. When you immediately pull out the big .45, you're asking for trouble, because once that thing gets going, it's like an eighteen-wheeler heading downhill—with no runaway pit in sight!

When you use everything you've got to please your wife, even helping her to achieve orgasm before you enter her, she probably won't care how fast you come. But when you focus only on your penis, and your penis doesn't perform, your wife is going to be very dissatisfied—and rightly so.

As a last-ditch effort for a special night, some of you guys might consider self-stimulation on the morning of a big "date." If you are consistently having trouble getting too frisky too quickly, then something as basic as masturbation in the morning before that evening with your wife might help. You shouldn't use masturbation as a substitute for sex with your wife—that's alienating and destructive. But if you're using it as preparation to better please your wife, I think it's acceptable, and sometimes wise.

Wives who want to help their husband in this regard can get creative as well. If you are habitually frustrated at how quickly your husband comes, plan a big date night, but the morning of that date, wake him up five minutes early with a quick "hand job." Then set the tone by saying, "That's just a preview of what's going to take place tonight, big boy!" Not too many men will complain that their wife wants them to have two orgasms in one day! Preparing your husband by getting that first one out of the way may help him last longer—

and ultimately please you better—later that night. And quick hand jobs truly don't require that much effort.

SINGING TOGETHER

I stated this at the start of this chapter, and I'll state it at the end: Most men get much more sexual pleasure out of watching their wife reach orgasm than they do experiencing their own. A man's orgasm usually pales in comparison to that experienced by his wife.

For this reason, I don't put much effort or concern into what some people refer to as simultaneous orgasms. Yes, it happens sometimes, and it can be kind of fun to both be in sexual ecstasy at exactly the same time—but even when it does occur, frankly, I feel like I'm missing out. I'm so caught up in what I'm experiencing that I don't get to see all that Sande is enjoying. And since I'm so attuned to her, that feels like a real loss.

My advice is, don't put too much thought or worry into achieving simultaneous orgasms. Please each other in a way that you know the other person wants to be pleased, and fully enjoy both of your orgasms.

But men, remember: Nice guys finish last! We don't need much time. Ten or fifteen seconds in a pinch will do. But a real lover will bring his wife along first, and if he thinks she desires it, he'll offer to give her a couple of extra crescendos to boot. Making love in this way is like a quarterback reading the defense—you've got to react immediately to what you see. If she is in intense pleasure and she wants you to enter and you don't, she's going to get mad. Conversely, if she's enjoying the way you're rubbing her clitoris and is near to climax, but you stop to enter her, she may become frustrated at you for that.

You won't find the key for those situations in a book, because your wife is absolutely unique in her sexual desires and pleasure. Besides that, she changes over time. Your wife on

Tuesday doesn't equal your wife on Saturday. And your wife on one Saturday in January won't equal your wife on a Saturday in June. Be creative, flexible, and learn to become an expert at making your wife feel good all over.

Now wipe that smile off your face and get busy! (How's that for a piece of homework?!)

7

Oral Delights

*F*or some reason, talk-show hosts are always eager to have a psychologist weigh in with his two bits. One day I was watching such a show with three "expert" fellow Christians. One of these guests, unfortunately, seemed more eager to discuss what a couple *can't* or *shouldn't* do than he was to discuss the great freedom and joy that God has designed for every married pair. He loudly denounced oral sex—even amongst married couples. Of course, he didn't have a Bible verse to stand on, but from the way he went on, you'd think he was looking the antichrist in the face!

My good friend Charlie Shedd, whom I've admired for years, leaned over and said, "Don't knock it until you've tried it!"

The "authority's" face went white, and I couldn't stop myself from laughing. Way to go, Charlie!

If God were to give me a magic wand that I could wave over couples across the country, I'd like a wand that instantly gives self-control and restraint to nonmarried couples (*Sha-bing!* Your zippers are locked until the wedding day!), and that correspondingly gives greater freedom and a sense of exploration to married couples (well, well, well—look at what we have here!). I really think married folks need the attitude talked about by my dermatologist. I've had a few "scares" in the skin cancer department, so the doc gave Sande and me an assignment. "Every six months, you and Sande need to explore each other's bodies—all over." He was talking about looking for moles that change color, stuff like that, but then he added with a twinkle in his eye, "You can make that really fun, can't you?"

You bet we can!

In the past, oral sex has often been looked on with disdain. In fact, many states still have laws on the books that outlaw this kind of activity. In my view, these are old-fashioned hangups. Consider instead the beautiful, almost reckless poetry presented in the Bible, in the Song of Songs. Yes, this is poetry, but it demonstrates a couple giving themselves fully to each other:

"His fruit is sweet to my taste." (2:3)[11]

"Let my lover come into his garden and taste its choice fruits." (4:16)

"I have come into my garden, my sister, my bride; I have gathered my myrrh with my spice. I have eaten my honeycomb and my honey; I have drunk my wine and my milk. Eat, O friends, and drink; drink your fill, O lovers." (5:1)

[11] All Scripture references in this section are from the New International Version.

"My lover has gone down to his garden, to the beds of spices, to browse in the gardens and to gather lilies. I am my lover's and my lover is mine; he browses among the lilies." (6:2-3)

"Your navel is a rounded goblet that never lacks blended wine." (7:2)

"I would give you spiced wine to drink, the nectar of my pomegranates." (8:2)

Many teachers believe that some of these passages directly relate to oral sex—stimulating a partner's genitals with your mouth. But even if they don't, they certainly speak of a loving abandonment and freedom to express passion in creative and thrilling ways. In fact, the Bible is silent on whether marital oral sex is immoral—which says to most Bible scholars that it must be okay. If God was so concerned about it, the reasoning goes, surely he would have forbidden it.

Think about it—if kissing someone on the lips is okay (and I don't know of anyone who objects to this on a moral basis) why is a kiss anywhere else "immoral"? Can a man then not kiss a woman's breasts? What about toes, or behind the knees, or other parts of the body known to be, in some people, sensitive to oral stimulation? Where do you draw the arbitrary line?

It certainly isn't a matter of hygiene. To put it bluntly, when a woman kisses a man's freshly washed penis, the woman's mouth has far more germs than the man's penis. If you're truly concerned about hygiene, forget mouth-to-mouth kissing and go straight to oral sex!

Having said this, no partner should ever be compelled to do something he or she finds either disagreeable or immoral—but few Christian leaders today would suggest there is anything wrong, biblically, with oral sex. And the disagreeable part can usually be overcome if both partners practice good hygiene before they come to bed.

Still, as a psychologist, I'm well aware that the older crowd tends to view oral sex as "taboo." Based on my own personal research and counseling practice of some thirty years, virtually all of the younger couples (in their twenties and thirties, whether married or unmarried) have oral sex as often as they have intercourse since it's "safer sex," while older couples (forties and above) tend to engage in oral sex much less frequently, if at all.

The irony of this is that the older a man gets, the more stimulation he needs! Oral sex can fit this bill perfectly. Another big advantage of oral sex for older couples is that it may take some pressure off a man's ability to get or maintain an erection. If a man knows he can please his partner regardless of his own erection, he's much less likely to worry about achieving one (which, ironically, makes it more likely that he *will*).

If oral sex is something you haven't tried in the past, you might consider adding it to tonight's menu.

TALKING ABOUT THE MENU

If you would like to try oral sex but aren't sure whether your spouse would be receptive, you have two options. One, you can bring it up in a gentle and loving talk: "Honey, I'd really like to try something new that will please you. What would you think if I started kissing you all over?"

Once your spouse receives this kind of caress, he or she may also be more inclined to give it.

Another option, though you need to be careful with this one, is to gradually progress toward oral sex in the heat of passion. Move down from your wife's breasts, kissing her stomach, and then maybe slipping down to her legs, slowly working your way back up her inner thighs. See how she responds. Does it seem that she wants you to go further, or is she becoming uncomfortable?

Don't rush anything, and if your wife is hesitant, *stop immediately*. The beauty of married sexuality is that you have your whole lives to grow and explore and enjoy each other. There's no hurry to experience any one activity. And it may be that one partner is never really willing to either give or receive oral sex. That's okay, too. There are many other ways a couple can enjoy sexual intimacy while still experiencing a variety of sexual activities.

For those women who want to serve up a special treat for their husbands, let's talk about making "Mr. Happy" smile.

MAKING MR. HAPPY REALLY HAPPY

Mr. Happy likes to be kissed. Nothing puts a smile on his face like a loving wife's oral caress. Each man has his individual preferences, but in general, here are a few guidelines.

Teasing is okay—for about ten seconds. Little tiny licks or a gentle brush of the tongue can be very arousing, but before too long, the man is going to want something far more direct. He's going to want you to cover his entire penis with your mouth. Many men will say the deeper the better.

This doesn't mean that once you have him in your mouth you can't come up for air. Feel free to back up, do some more licking, light blowing, and whatnot, but don't wait too long to go back.

Here's something many women don't realize: The underside of the penis is more sensitive than the top side. One long, luxurious lick here in the teasing phase and your husband will be grabbing his pillow and wriggling around in delight.

If you're new to this, the first question you'll probably want to ask is, "What about my teeth?" The short answer is, "Yes, teeth hurt!" You'll want to curl your lips over them and be gentle—especially if you wear braces.

The second question I'm often asked is, "Am I doing it right?" Listen, you're not being viewed by Olympic judges here! "I would have given them a 10, but her toes weren't curled, so I'm scoring them with a 9.5." It's not a matter of being correct or incorrect as much as it is whether your husband is enjoying the process. To find out the answer to that, you'll need to ask *him*, not me! Don't take it personally if, initially, he says, "A little softer, a little slower, a little harder . . ." Nobody is born with the skills to be a good lover, so you needn't be embarrassed that it takes a little practice.

A third question invariably concerns the climax. To some women, the thought of swallowing any ejaculate is distasteful. There is nothing inherently unhealthy about a man's semen, and the amount expelled during an ejaculation is relatively small. But if the thought of tasting it is repellent to you, simply pull your mouth away before your husband reaches orgasm. In time, you'll be able to tell when this is by feeling the contractions in his penis. A caring husband can also warn you if he knows of your reluctance. While you may pull back with your mouth, keep stimulating him with your hand; it will certainly be a letdown for your husband if you stop all stimulation right at the moment he'll enjoy it most.

Sometimes a man really enjoys having his wife make eye contact while she kisses him. Remember, men tend to be more visual. If you don't mind having a soft light in the background, or even candles glowing, your husband may enjoy the sight as much as he enjoys the feel. This may necessitate your holding your hair back so it doesn't act like a curtain.

While we usually refer to this as "oral sex" for lack of a better phrase, this doesn't mean that only the tongue needs to be involved. In fact, you can greatly increase your spouse's pleasure by bringing your hands and fingers into play. If your mouth gets tired, you can take a short break while stroking your husband with your hand. Or you can use mouth and hands together, caressing your husband in his most intimate places while you plant kisses all over him.

Some women I have counseled have been surprised that they have learned to really enjoy the practice of giving oral sex. It's no longer a duty, but a true pleasure. When a woman shows her own enjoyment in pleasuring her husband, she's giving him an unusually intense gift. Nothing will excite your man more than to know that you're excited—particularly as you do something to arouse him.

MAKING YOUR WIFE BITE THE PILLOW

It might surprise some of you men that when women masturbate, almost all of them stimulate the clitoris; relatively few of them insert something into their vagina.

What does this tell you? It reveals that the most stimulating part of the female genitalia is on the outside. Don't get me wrong—women enjoy the sensation of having their husband's penis inside them. But when it comes to sexual stimulation, they prefer to be rubbed and caressed more than penetrated.

Think about it: There is no softer or gentler way to stimulate your wife than with your tongue. If she truly prefers being caressed, what more able instrument do you possess than your tongue?

I can't think of one!

Even so, some women are just as hesitant about letting a husband perform oral sex on them as they are about performing oral sex on their husbands. "I can understand her not wanting to do it to me," some husbands have said to me, "but why wouldn't she want to receive it?"

Keep in mind that there is no more physically intimate act you can perform on your wife than oral sex. Those past politicians who tried to suggest oral sex isn't really "sex" weren't kidding anyone; we all know better. The woman is as vulnerable as she'll ever be, and she may be thinking, *Will he find this disgusting? What if I smell bad, or taste bad? Is he really hating this?* Filled with these thoughts, it's difficult for some women to just lie back and enjoy the experience.

In fact, *most* of the women I talk to confess that early on in their marriage, they didn't want oral sex performed on them, and when it did happen, they were so self-conscious that it wasn't particularly enjoyable. Once they get over this psychological hurdle, these same women often love oral sex—the longer the better. But it truly is a hurdle for many women.

Because of this—again, speaking as a psychologist here—this is one instance where a husband's pleasure matters as much as his wife's. You are giving to her when you allay these fears by assuring her, verbally and otherwise, that this is something you enjoy.

For the sake of both partners, have your wife take a bath or shower before she comes to bed. If she feels clean, she'll be less self-conscious. You'll want to take your time, men, going from first base to home plate. Though you might not mind it if your wife were to wake you up with a mouthful, your wife is normally going to want you to work your way there.

Kiss her behind the ears, work your way down her neck, spend some time around her breasts, don't forget that lovely spot inside the elbow, and then teasingly skip over her midsection and work your way down her legs. That spot behind the knees can drive a woman wild if you know how to lick it just right. Such soft places can come alive with feeling during a leisurely season of lovemaking. As you change direction, you may find that there's something about gently kissing a woman's inner thighs that makes her slide downwards! If you do this right, slowly working your way back up north, your wife will be practically (or maybe, if you're lucky, literally) begging you to kiss her in the right place. When you've got her really wanting it, and you provide that soft, sensual kiss, you can make her start biting the pillow for fear she'll wake up the kids.

Here's a particularly nice position for this: Facing her feet, slide your right hand under your wife (under her bottom). Your fingers are right there, waiting to do a little dance on your wife's genitalia, and your mouth has full access to her most pleasurable regions; the edges of her clitoris and the folds of the labia are all there for your fingers and tongue to work together.

Men, it's all about setting the tone and taking your time to arrive. If you get your wife ready, she'll forget where she is and become lost in where you're taking her. You'd be surprised at some of the things a Sunday-school-teaching wife will do and say in the heat of such passion. When your wife is aroused, the whole area will be sensitive. Don't ignore anything, and vary the motions of your tongue. You can alternate licking, gently pulling (with your *lips, not your teeth!*), and kissing. Above all, remember this credo: *Gently, men, gently.* The most common complaint in this department is that the man is too harsh and ends up hurting, rather than pleasuring, his wife. This is especially true as he senses his wife is heating up and he gets carried away. Your tongue needs to be insistent, but soft. Listen to your wife's reactions. She may be nervous about saying "Ow!"—not wanting to hurt your feelings—so look for nonverbal cues.

Don't just sit on your hands, by the way. Let your fingers touch wherever your tongue can't reach. The combined stimulation can send your wife writhing. Reach up and caress her breasts, or stimulate her clitoris with your fingers while you lick lower. Or, gently kiss her clitoris with your mouth while you penetrate her vagina with one or two fingers, perhaps reaching for "her" spot.

Having laid out the possible pleasures of oral sex, I want to add that men or women should never, *ever* force their mate to do anything they don't want to do. Remember that verse:

"Love does not demand its own way." If your spouse—for whatever reason—finds the thought of oral sex to be disagreeable, distasteful, or immoral, it's wrong of you to make him or her feel guilty or to continue pressing your spouse to "give in."

SOME TREATS TO ORAL SEX

If you're already well-versed in the arts of oral sex, here are a few special "treats" you may not have thought of:

- Try eating a few Altoids before kissing your partner, or let a cough drop linger in your mouth while you take care of business. The "menthol" from your tongue will transfer a very pleasurable sensation.
- Another good idea is to put a cup of hot tea near the bed. Keep taking sips. Not only does it make your partner taste good, but that extra warm tongue will drive him or her crazy.
- Hum while you pleasure your partner.
- Wives, remember that husbands are very visual. If you can let him see what you are doing, and perhaps even put your hair up, he'll be so very thankful. Occasional eye contact is a powerful aphrodisiac!

I can't wait to see the mail I'll receive about this chapter!

8

For Men Only

*I*n the next two chapters, I want to talk to each spouse individually. I'd still like to encourage women to read the chapter for men, and men to read the chapter for women, as reading it together can give you a lot to discuss. The issues I'll be touching on are the issues that come up most frequently when sex is discussed in the counseling room.

CLEAN MATTERS
Guys, one of the things I hear most frequently from women is that you come to bed smelling like sweaty gym socks, and then you want your wife to get up close and intimate with just about every part of your body.

I don't think so.

Years ago we did a radio show on hygiene. I prefer not to know a show's topic ahead of time because I like to approach it from a fresh perspective—just like the listener does. I don't want the show to sound contrived or artificial. So, as is my custom, just before we went on the air I asked the producer what we were going to talk about.

"Hygiene and sex," he said.

"No, really," I said.

"Hygiene and sex," he repeated.

"You're serious."

"I am."

"Well, let me go on record before this show fails that this may be the stupidest idea we've ever come up with."

I couldn't have been more wrong. The phones lit up as soon as the topic was explained, and the calls kept coming full blast throughout the entire hour. We received a tremendous response because unclean husbands who don't shower, brush their teeth, or prepare themselves before they come to bed really turn women off—and finally these women were able to talk about it.

Let me put it this way: At 10 P.M., your beard stubble feels like a coarse grade of sandpaper. All that tension you felt at the office has been sweating through your skin, staining your armpits and making your feet smell like a compost pile. And though you have enough power to bring a woman to ecstasy and back with just your index finger, if you never use an emery board and smooth out those fingernails, you can make her squeal for a far different reason.

Rachel Herz, a professor of experimental psychology at Brown University, published a study in which she asked 332 college students a series of questions about what attracts them to the opposite sex. The female students consistently said that smell attracted them to a man even more than visual cues.[12]

[12]Didi Gluck, "The Scent-Sex Connection," Redbook, November 2000, 142.

In other words, even if you look "buff," you're not going to get far if you smell like a dead rat.

So learn how to use a bar of soap. Take a shower before you hop into bed if you've had a busy or stressful day, or if you want your wife to get particularly close (you know what I'm talking about). If you make your wife's experience more pleasant, she'll be more accommodating.

And remember: Your own "sniff" isn't a good-enough gauge. A woman's sense of smell is physiologically more acute than a man's. So even though you think you don't smell, that doesn't mean your wife's superior nose isn't picking up an offensive signal.

SUBTLE IS SUPERIOR

For some reason, most of us men still mentally reside somewhere around the caveman age when it comes to romance. By that, I mean we still think women like to be grabbed, pinched, and mauled.

Occasionally, if the setting is right, a little aggressive and playful "mauling" might be welcome, but 90 percent of the time, a woman likes her man's touches to be much more subtle. She doesn't want you to grab her breasts like you'd squeeze a tennis ball to see if it's flat; she doesn't like you to slap her rear end as if she had just hit a home run. She wants your touch to be *subtle*. If you really want to spend all day "warming up" your wife, you need to take a much softer approach and pay attention to less obvious areas.

Here are some actual comments given by women as they talked about ways that men in the past have made their hearts melt:

"Brushing a strand of hair from my face."

"Brushing my hair."

"Having his hands tangled in my hair."

"Kissing me behind the ear."

"Touching my face."

"When he sits close to me and puts his arm around my shoulder."

"When he has his hand on my thigh when we sit next to each other at the movies, at dinner, on the couch watching a video."

One woman gave this testimony: "We were on our evening walk. We stopped at the top of the hill and when I turned toward him, he ran his hand along my cheek. Then he stroked my hair. Suddenly, I wanted him."[13]

There's not a single, "I just *love* it when he suddenly grabs my crotch!" in the bunch. But notice how many women referred to their man running his hands through her hair. When's the last time you did that?

The difference here is that while many men are prone to be *sexually* oriented in their thoughts, women tend to be *sensually* oriented.[14] Immediately going for a woman's private parts or participating in an unannounced mammary mauling isn't sensual; it's sexual (though not very, at least for the woman!).

LET YOUR FINGERS DO THE TALKING

Most women generally won't experience an orgasm through intercourse alone. I don't care if your first name is Don and your last name is Juan—physiologically, intercourse seems designed for one purpose: to get the man to deposit his sperm. It's an ideal setting for *your* orgasm, but not necessarily for your partner's, so slow down—you're going to have to get your hands involved.

Most women need to have their clitoris stimulated in order to reach orgasm. The clitoris is a small fleshy knob that can be found just above the opening of the vagina. Your wife actually

---

[13]Lucy Sanna with Kathy Miller, *How to Romance the Woman You Love—The Way She Wants You To!* (New York: Gramercy Books, 1998 edition), 70-71.
[14]Sanna with Miller, *How to Romance*, 73.

has two sets (inner and outer) of fleshy lips, called "labia." The outer labia are covered with hair. The inner labia form an upside-down V that looks like this: ∧. The clitoris is that fleshy knob right at the top of the point; it's surrounded by a hood. When a woman isn't fully aroused, the "bump" of the clitoris is usually buried in folds of skin.

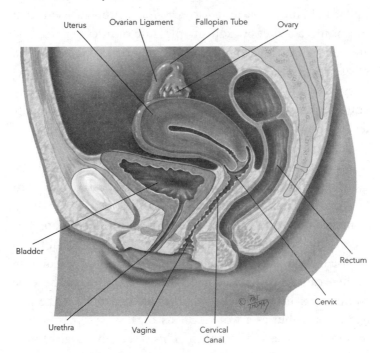

Like penises, clitorises vary in size. Some protrude through the lips of the labia and are easy to find; others are smaller. When a sensitive and loving husband does his job right and tenderly arouses his wife, the clitoris usually gets larger, making it easier to find.

This might shock some of you men, but a woman's clitoris is actually, on average, about nine inches long. You only see about a tenth of that, of course; the rest of it is nestled inside the woman's body. The pleasurable part that sticks out is part of a much larger main, sort of like a love iceberg with just the tip available to the, er, naked eye (pun fully intended). The other eight-plus inches that you don't see stretch back into the shape of a wishbone inside the pelvis.[15] This makes the entire area very receptive to sexual touch.

The concentration of blood vessels and nerves found in the tip of the clitoris make it *hypersensitive* to touch. Men, that means it is a center of exquisite pleasure or intense pain. You are dealing with an extremely sensitive instrument. Above all, please understand that the clitoris isn't a crank that leads to ecstasy. Nor is it like a motorcycle handlebar accelerator, where you just keep turning and turning and turning and literally feel the power explode beneath you. The clitoris is a very sensitive organ that needs to be handled with care. Sometimes indirect handling is the very best kind. A direct touch might be painful, depending on the woman, in which case you'll want to move the labia around the clitoris to indirectly stimulate it. Some women need to have the clitoris lubricated before they have it touched, and many like it rubbed in a circular motion.

You'll also want to vary the intensity, location, and duration of these caresses. What feels good for two minutes may become painful after three. Usually a lighter teasing touch is the preferred route—but as a woman nears orgasm, she may want a more vigorous and direct touch. This is the advantage of married sex—over time, you'll learn what your spouse prefers.

Just about every sexual position allows a man to have at least one hand free. Whether you're on top or she's on top, whether you're behind with her on her knees, or the two of you are spooning, you can reach around and oh, so carefully, find that tender little friend. You need to become very familiar with this little knob if you ever want to make your wife feel truly satisfied.

[15]Cited in Andrew Levin, "Mysteries of the Cligeva," *Men's Journal*, February 2001, 49.

Women, let me add a little note here specifically for you: *Help* your husband pleasure you. Every woman is different; every clitoris, so to speak, prefers a unique touch. Instead of making your husband guess, or making him feel stupid or inadequate because his touch isn't right, take the time to lovingly guide him.

Since this can be a sensitive issue, try to use positive motivation. As soon as he stumbles on something that works, be effusive: "Oh yes, honey, just like that. That's perfect." "Oh, you're making me so wet." "Oh—right there; that's the spot. Yes!" "Oh please don't stop, oh, please, yes, that's right, please don't stop!"

If he gets a little carried away, don't be shy about asking him to ease off: "Easy, honey, it's a little sensitive there." Over time, you may feel comfortable enough to guide your husband's hand. Remember, you're the only one who truly knows what a touch feels like on your body. Your husband can look for clues, but you'll make it a lot easier on him if you'll be a little more vocal.

THEY'RE NOT AS SENSITIVE AS YOU THOUGHT

The areola—the dark, nipple part of the breast—isn't as sensitive as men often think. In fact, some researchers from Boston suggest that the areola is about two to three times *less* sensitive than a woman's index finger.

That *doesn't* mean you can treat the nipple like a car radio dial; but it does mean you might need to be a little firmer to get a touch that your wife will appreciate.

Having said this, remember once again that all women's breasts are different—not just in size, but in sensitivity as well. Some women can reach climax merely by having their breasts fondled. Others won't even come close following that route.

MAKE LOVE TO HER

Women know men tend to be more interested in sex than they are. Just because you're sexually excited doesn't mean anything to your wife other than the fact that you like sex and want her to "service" you.

That's why it's so important to make sure your wife knows you are making love *to her*. You want her to know your desire isn't simply for an orgasm (though if she's offering, you're not planning to turn her down . . .), but that you truly desire *her*. She's the only one you want to be with.

How do you do that? Rushed foreplay, vigorous thrusting, and then flopping off her and falling immediately to sleep isn't the best recipe. Let me tell you what some women say makes them feel special during sex:

"When he talks to me during lovemaking, letting me know that he wants me and why and how I turn him on. Tell me more!"

"Eye contact. When we're kissing. When we're loving. I love to see the expression in his eyes, because when he's loving me his expression is always so caring."

"When making love, he touches my face, says my name, plays with my hair. It makes me feel that he's glad he's with *me*."[16]

I think you get the point by now: Find ways to let your wife know you desire *her* more than you desire sex. Make sex *personal, passionate,* and *relational.*

THE "HER" SPOT

Just about everybody these days has heard about the famous "G" spot, which gets its name from Dr. Graffenberg, the doctor who first described it half a century ago. For the woman, the G spot is, anatomically speaking, her urethral sponge. Sorry if that spoils some of the mystery, but there you have it.

Though women vary as to the sensitivity of their G spot, it

---

[16]Sanna with Miller, *How to Romance,* 81.

is certainly something that the sensitive spouse will want to become familiar with. But don't get too carried away with it. Instead of the G spot, I like to talk to couples about what I call the "her" spot.

What I've found is that the "her" spot *moves*. It doesn't matter what you call it—the G spot, the M spot, the Z spot, or the hot spot—on Tuesday it's here, but on Saturday it's over there. My wife is German, but I think she's part leopard, because her spots change! They're transient little suckers, and if I become too obsessed with something I read about in a magazine article, I'm going to miss her spot.

Our job as men is to figure out what makes our own wife tick. What makes your wife tick may not be what makes my wife tick.

But just so you're fully educated and feel you got what you paid for in this book, let's go over what the famous doctor had to say about a spot that's supposed to make your wife's toes curl.

First off, men, let me caution you—the G spot isn't a trigger that can be pushed to set off fireworks at will. You've got to work your way toward it. If you jam some fingers up there and start fishing around, you're liable to turn your wife into a killer whale instead of a purring kitten. Do your work first, and once your wife is already aroused, *gently* insert one or two fingers (your palm should be facing *you*) into her vagina. This next part varies from woman to woman, but in general, about one or two inches above the vagina's opening, on the front wall, you'll eventually feel a small spot that has a few ridges, or that feels a little rougher than the surrounding skin. Since you're touching the urethra, your wife may be worried that she needs to urinate—but soon, if you keep applying gentle pressure, that urge will collapse into a very pleasant sensation. You'll know you've hit the jackpot when the moans soon follow.

You may find it easier to locate your wife's G spot by having her lie on her stomach and open her legs to you. In this case, you'll be pressing down with your fingers. Try rubbing up and down as well as side-to-side, and encourage your wife to give you some feedback. This spot feels different for every woman, so you'll need to learn what feels best for your wife. It's even better if you bring two hands into play, stimulating the clitoris at the same time that you rub the G spot.

To hit the G spot during intercourse, it's often best to put the wife on top. The man should lay back with his knees raised, providing something for the wife to lean back against. With practice, she'll be able to direct her husband's penis to exactly the right spot.

Then hold on.

An alternative is for the husband to enter his wife from behind, consciously attempting to caress his wife's G spot with his penis. This will take more than aimless thrusting, of course; it will require a sensitive effort on the man's part.

FREQUENCY FIGHTS

"So," I said to the man seated in front of me, who had three kids and had been married for eighteen years, "what is it you'd really like to do in bed?"

"Sex would be nice," he replied.

I should have been more specific.

When a couple comes to me talking about problems with their love life, "frequency fights" are one of the most common disagreements. Though I've spoken to a number of women who desire sex more often than their husbands do, typically, men feel like they're having to beg for about half as much sex as they'd like.

Don't resent it when your wife doesn't want sex as often as you do; the difference is usually hormonal. Your wife doesn't have your testosterone coursing through her body so, you can't expect her to have the same desire that you do or fault her for not having it. While some things can improve desire, it's what we do with desire or the lack of it that we can control—not the desire itself.

Most men need to "dial it back" a little bit. By that I mean stop expecting your wife to meet your sexual needs perfectly. Settle for improvement. The perfect sex life you have in your mind probably doesn't exist; it's far more helpful to work toward something that's better than to fight over an ideal two people will probably never achieve.

I'll be a little vulnerable here. Sometimes authors get lost in the ideal and present unrealistic pictures. I'm a forty-eight-hour man myself; if it's been more than thirty-six hours or so, sex becomes very, very important to me. But you know what? Having sex every forty-eight hours rarely happens in the Leman household. It would be an unusual week for Sande and me to get together three or four times. With my travel schedule, raising five children, and my wife's store of refurbished antiques, Shabby Hattie, we simply don't have the time and energy to have sex as often as I would like to have it—but we still have a good sex life. Why? Because I don't let what *could be* wreck what we *do* have.

FEMALE FANTASIES

Females *do* have fantasies. But they will never equal male fantasies. Yet, fortunately for you, most female fantasies are actually within reach of the average guy. Two women writers did a survey in which they asked women to describe their romantic fantasies. The answers were encouraging: "You may be pleased to learn that not one fantasy mentioned being decked in diamonds, swathed in mink, or stolen away on a private yacht to Fantasy Island. No, the fantasies women of all ages across the country described were very attainable by the everyday, nine-to-five guy."[17]

[17]Sanna with Miller, *How to Romance*, 147.

These fantasies included outdoor sports, shopping, musical performances, and good restaurants. The main key to these "fantasies" is that the women wanted the men to handle all the child-care and booking details. So often the man says, "Honey, let's go away for the weekend," and then leaves it to her to find the hotel, make the dinner reservations, locate someone to watch the kids, etc.

If your wife's fantasy involves dinner, go for an intimate setting. Smaller rooms and booths with candlelight are to be preferred over a loud, barnlike atmosphere. Look for places that use cloth napkins and play slow and soft music. Go in style; get dressed up a bit, and maybe buy your wife a new piece of jewelry or a new dress to wear. And once you're there, keep in mind that your conversation will make or break this dinner. Sanna and Miller suggest the following:[18]

She Wants to Hear About:
- How wonderful she looks
- How you miss her
- How good it is to be with her
- Plans for your future together
- What you like about your relationship
- Plans for her future (to meet her personal dreams, goals, etc.)
- Her interests (encourage her in them)
- How you met (reminisce about the wonderful beginnings)
- Why she's special to you
- Positive things about the restaurant
- Her accomplishments
- Her day
- Her ideas
- The appreciation you have for all she does

She Doesn't Want to Hear About:
- The kids, the in-laws
- The office
- Looking forward to something that doesn't involve her
- Anything negative, anything you don't like about *anything*
- Topics you disagree on that may cause an argument
- Chores
- Expenses, bills, taxes
- Problems of today
- Other women, past or present
- Negative things about the restaurant
- Your accomplishments
- Your day
- Your ideas
- The difficulties you had in planning this great date

[18]Sanna with Miller, *How to Romance*, 158.

Of course, some women *do* want to hear about your day, but only after you've taken an interest in theirs. Keep the focus positive, on her, and relational.

"But wait a minute, Dr. Leman," some of you men are saying. "What's so sexy about this?"

Ah, my dear friend, you've made the ultimate male error. You've assumed that "fantasy" and "sex" are combined in the female mind. That's not necessarily true. But you know what? Fulfill this fantasy, and your wife's interest in sex with you will increase about a hundredfold—as long as she feels secure that you're not doing this just so that you can expect a big "payoff" in return.

A survey asked women to fill in the blank: "If he were more romantic, I would be more inclined to . . ." The answers were:

1. "Be excited to be with him"
2. "Keep myself looking attractive"
3. "Find out what he wants; try to help him fulfill his needs"
4. "Stay with him rather than find a new partner"
5. "Be in a good mood around him"
6. "Attend to his sexual needs"[19]

Out of all the billions of men on the face of the earth, your wife chose you. Why do you think that was? Was it because she thought the way you acted during dating is the way you'd act while you were married?

That's pretty reasonable, when you think about it.

Are you taking your wife for granted? Are you still doing the things you did to "court" her and "date" her? Would you have shown up for a college dance smelling like 10-30 motor oil? Then why do you come to bed stinking like that?

The best way to improve your sex life, including your wife's desire for you, is to focus on the other 95 percent of your marriage and build that up.

[19]Sanna with Miller, *How to Romance*, 189.

9

For Women Only

A woman I know decided to apply some of the principles I talk about in this book and really surprise her husband. She wanted to do something shocking. And since her husband had been away for an entire month on a business trip, she came up with a great idea to reward him for his faithfulness.

To get herself in the mood, she took a nice, long bubble bath. She shaved her legs, sprayed on her husband's favorite perfume, and then put on a garter belt, stockings, a trench coat—and nothing else. She then drove to the airport, parked the car, and walked inside, hoping to meet her husband at the gate.

She forgot about security. As soon as she walked through the machine, it gave a loud *BEEEEP!*

And that's when she remembered the metal garter belt she was wearing.

Her face went whiter than the clean sheets she had just put on the bed. She looked behind her to see an elderly couple, a young businessman, and an impatient family waiting to get through. What could she do?

The security officer tried to be helpful. "I'm sure it's just the belt on your coat, ma'am. Why don't you just take off your coat and put it through the machine by itself?"

"Take my coat off?" she asked in a panic.

"Or at least the belt."

By this time, all the blood in her body had drained out of her head. Her hands were numb and cold as she slipped the belt off and then clasped her coat shut with an iron grip, praying as fiercely as she had ever prayed that the metal garter belt wouldn't set off the machine once again.

She walked back through the machine, ready to die of embarrassment. Never had the sound of silence sounded so wonderful to a young wife. She quickly grabbed her coat belt, slipped it back around her, and met her husband at the gate.

Of course, he thought the story was hilarious—and he appreciated the gesture even more than this woman might realize. Even so, she warned him, "Don't *ever* expect a surprise like this again!"

WHY NOT?

Receiving and giving spontaneous gestures, like the above, can work wonders for your marriage. In fact, the bulk of what I want to say in this chapter is this: Why *not* now, and why *not* here?

Has your husband ever come up behind you, cupping a breast as you put mascara on your eyes, only to have his hand slapped away with a curt, "Not now!"

Why *not* now?

How long does it take to caress a breast? Ten seconds?

Twenty seconds? Can you really not give your husband that amount of time?

I know what you're thinking: *You don't understand, Dr. Leman. If I let him touch my breast, I'll be on my back looking up at the ceiling in ten seconds flat. My clothes will be thrown all over the floor, my hair will get messed up, and I'll have to redo my makeup. Then I'll be late for work.*

Sometimes this might be the case. As a rare circumstance, I might even say being late to work once or twice a year could be just what your marriage needs! But many times your husband just wants a quick feel. So next time surprise him by turning around and getting a quick feel of your own.

There's such a huge difference between a wife who slaps a man's hands away and one who giggles mischievously, even engaging in one or two minutes of light petting, only to whisper in his ear, "This sounds so delicious, but unfortunately, I really do have to get ready for work. Let's save it for tonight, when you'll get all you want and more." The second woman will have fulfilled her husband, even while staying clothed and keeping her hair in place. The first wife will have deflated her husband and eroded his masculinity, all for the sake of sixty to ninety seconds.

That's a costly minute.

WHY NOT NOW?

Men are more fragile than most women realize. They want to be the pleaser, and their feelings get hurt far more easily than many women will ever know. Men don't just think about golf and killing deer—in fact, the reason they may seem obsessed by those things is because they often don't feel loved at home and so run out-of-doors to escape.

Do you want to give your husband a special treat? The next time he comes behind you and gently takes a breast in his hand, expecting you to slap him away, let him keep it there for a few seconds. When he finally pulls away, call out after him and say, "Hey!" in a forceful voice.

When you've got his attention, say, "You forgot the other one."

My faithful readers, if you do this, it will be one conversation your husband may never forget.

I want to help you understand how a man thinks. When I see Sande bending over to unload the dishwasher, I'll say something like, "Do you want to know what I'm thinking right now?"

"No, Lemey, I *don't* want to know what you're thinking; go find something to do."

Women often don't get it that the mere sight of them bending over may do something profound to a man. We're visual creatures, and we're given visual clues all day long. Combined with the testosterone coursing through our bodies, that makes many of us live in a heightened state of sexual alert.

Now, here's another scenario. If I say the same thing to Sande when she's bending over the dishwasher, she might say, "Lemey, Mr. Happy has this habit of getting himself all excited at times where there's not a chance he's going to get lucky. But I'll tell you what: Mr. Happy is going to get quite a workout tonight. I'm looking forward to it. In fact, there's nothing I'm looking forward to more."

When Sande does this, it's even better than her immediately giving in! You know why? She's using the power of anticipation, and anticipation is even better than participation, emotionally, for a man.

Does that surprise you? Think about it. How long does participation last? Ten minutes for a quickie? Twenty minutes on average? Forty-five to sixty minutes if you really take your time?

But a wife who tells her husband, "Tonight's the night!" is giving her husband an *entire day* of pleasure. Twenty minutes will hardly go by without your husband thinking of you, imagining you, wanting you. Doesn't that sound wonderful? To have your husband thinking loving and affectionate thoughts about you all day long?

The words you choose are really important. When your husband is about to leave the house and he comes up to you to give you a perfunctory kiss, if you surprise him by giving him a real kiss—practically cleaning his bicuspids in the process—and then say, "I've got plans for you later, buddy, so hurry home from work," you're going to be on someone's mind all day long.

WHY NOT HERE?

Another famous saying women throw at their husbands is, "Not here."

Why not here? Who says lovemaking is fit only for the bedroom? Why not be a little adventurous?

I'm not suggesting you make love in the middle of a mall or at your daughter's baccalaureate ceremony, but hey, if your husband starts getting frisky in the kitchen and nobody else is home, there are actually quite a few interesting items in just about every kitchen that can be used on a body instead of on bread.

Think about it!

I was doing an autograph party at a store that had also invited the late comedian Steve Allen. Both of us were talking with people as we signed books. The book I was signing was entitled *Sex Begins in the Kitchen.*

Steve and I watched as an elderly couple strolled by, arm in arm, obviously in love with each other, but also obviously at least in their eighties. The woman, with snow-white hair and granny glasses, looked at the display of my book, boldly proclaiming that sex begins in the kitchen. She turned toward her husband and said, "Not in our house; too many windows!"

Steve and I both had a good belly laugh at that one, it was so funny.

Look, I'm not asking you to be immodest, and I'm certainly not suggesting you should do anything that could get you arrested. But if the kids are gone, and your backyard is private, or if the living-room drapes are closed and your husband is suddenly behind you—well, in those cases, just ask yourself, "Why not here?" If you can't think of a good reason not to, maybe you should make the first move!

GETTING COMFORTABLE WITH MR. HAPPY

I've said in another book that a man's best friend isn't a dog— and that friendship starts early.

True story: A young mother was giving her three-year-old son a bath when he looked up and said, "Mommy, I love my penis."

Flustered, the young mom launched into an anatomy lesson. "Well, honey, God made us, and he gave us elbows and fingers and toes and knees and ears and feet—and every part is just as important as every other part."

The boy didn't say a word but listened patiently to his mom's lesson on the wonders of the human body. When she finished, he said, "But, Mommy, I still like my penis the best."[20]

"Mr. Happy"—as I prefer to call him—is someone you're going to have to become comfortable with if you want to please your husband. This shouldn't be too difficult; after all, it's been a long-held opinion of mine that Mr. Happy is adorable (though my wife doesn't always agree). Please don't say what I've actually heard that some wives say when they first see their husband's genitals: "That's the ugliest thing I ever saw in

[20]Dr. Kevin Leman, *Making Sense of the Men in Your Life* (Nashville: Thomas Nelson, 2000), 43–44.

my life!" Even if that's true, it's probably best to keep it to yourself.

If your husband is young, in his twenties or early thirties, you can often get by with merely winking at Mr. Happy, and he'll dutifully raise himself in an honorary salute. But as your husband ages, you'll need to learn the art of stimulating a penis. Since so few women receive actual sexual instruction, here's a quick primer on pleasuring your husband's most cherished member.

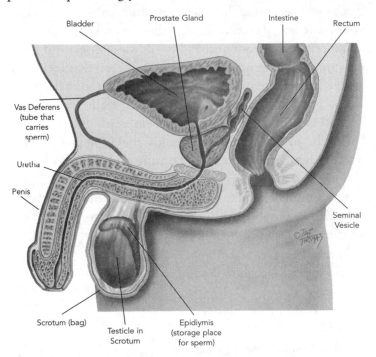

For starters, the most sensitive part of a man's penis is usually the underside of the shaft and the head. Pay particular attention to the ridge on the bottom of the head. There's a little indentation on that ridge that is hypersensitive. A tongue or light lick here and your husband may hit the ceiling.

The penis is surrounded with many different sensors. Stroking the shaft creates one feeling, and often is a good way to bring a man to erection. Focusing on the more sensitive head is more intense and often the place to create a climax. In time, you'll learn how to make your man hard without bringing him "over the edge." It's a skillful lover indeed who can bring her husband to the peak of sexual ecstasy, but then know when to back off to prolong the pleasure, only to bring him right back up the mountain once again. Different strokes, different places to touch, different caresses (some light, some firm; some fast, some slow) all create different experiences for your husband. At certain times in the lovemaking experience, you'll notice that your husband needs more direct and forceful stimulation; at other times, you'll discern that too much more direct stimulation will lead him straight to orgasm.

Get good at exploring your husband, really knowing his whole body. It's not just women who enjoy foot rubs and back rubs and head rubs. Men enjoy these touches too (just don't bring this up around his hunting buddies).

Some women have asked me if men have their own G spot. A few researchers have gotten pretty specific, but when a woman asks me about this, I take a different approach. "You want to know your husband's G spot?"

"Yeah."

"All right, think about a spotted leopard."

"Okay."

"Got that in your mind?"

"Yeah."

"Now just take your pick!"

Men just like to be touched, and all spots work pretty well. Just touch them and they're going to respond.

ALWAYS READY

To the chagrin of many a wife, Mr. Happy doesn't live by a schedule. In fact, Mr. Happy doesn't even know what a schedule is. He also has a very short memory.

For example, let's say you and your husband had a nice, long, and leisurely session of lovemaking the night before. The next morning your husband is watching you stretch to put a book up on a bookcase. It's Saturday morning and you're just working around the house, so you didn't bother to put on a bra. As you stretch, your breasts move provocatively inside your T-shirt.

Now you're probably thinking like a woman: *We had sex last night, I haven't showered yet, I'm wearing grubby clothes. The seduction factor has to be 1 on a scale of 1 to 10.*

Yet you notice that within seconds your husband has come up to give you a hug from behind and you're suddenly very, very aware that Mr. Happy is not exactly "resting."

You think, *What's wrong here? We just did it last night!*

Sorry, but this is all about a relationship; there is no scoreboard or contest. This fact may be particularly difficult for my firstborn female readers, who tend to want everything to operate on a schedule. Good luck trying to put Mr. Happy on a schedule.

If you talk to fulfilled couples, you'll hear the word *spontaneity*. Since men are driven by sight, a quick glance at a woman in her underwear or getting out of the shower can be enough of a trigger—especially if it has been a couple of days. In such instances, your husband may not care if church starts in fifteen minutes or if he has an important meeting at the office. One of the most famous movie scenes ever (which I haven't witnessed, but I've read much about it) was an early Sharon Stone movie in which she apparently took a little extra time crossing her legs. Men across the nation were mesmerized; I'm sure women watching that scene thought, *What's the big deal? She crossed her legs. It was over before you knew what was happening.*

Trust me, women—just a glance is all it takes.

It's not just sight that will catch us. A woman can make many men's heads turn simply by choosing the right perfume. Men can become puppy dogs, utterly conquered by certain aromas.

"Will you marry me?"

"I don't even know you!"

"It doesn't matter—if you'll always smell this good, I want to be your husband."

I remember after a few years of marriage, Sande said to me, "It sure doesn't take much to get you going, Leman." The inexperienced woman may think, *What have I gotten myself into?* I talk to young wives all the time who are truly shocked at the frequency and duration of their husband's sexual interest. Some have told me that they thought if they just gave in and had sex five days in a row, their husband would be "cured." Not a chance. He might be smiling this week, but next week, he's still going to be interested.

This "always on" mentality men have isn't a conspiracy; it's how God made us. Keep reminding yourself of this: "God made my husband that way." God thinks it's important that your husband be chemically drawn to you and motivated to get physically close to you on a regular and consistent basis.

I don't know how many women I have gently chided with the words, "Please don't fault your husband for being a man."

"What do you mean?"

"If you wanted someone who talks about and loves to do all the same things you do, you should have stayed single and cultivated female roommates. But you married a man who has different likes and different needs, and among those needs is sex."

NEW ATTITUDE

More important than your breast size, more important than your waist size, more important than the length of your legs is your attitude. The vast majority of men would rather have a wife who's a little on the plain side but has a sexually available attitude than a drop-dead gorgeous woman who treats her husband like ice, constantly freezing him out.

A positive attitude also means appreciating and respecting

your husband. That's what men want. Unfortunately, it has become culturally acceptable to bash men and to transform the male species into narrow creatures who think only through their penis. That's not true; in fact, sexually fulfilled men think about sex far less than sexually frustrated men! If your husband is obsessed with sex, it might be because he doesn't feel that he's experiencing it enough!

Women need to be willing to stand up for their husbands, even in conversations with girlfriends. There's nothing that will make a man prouder and fall more in love with his wife than to hear that she stood up for him and his species during a heated gabfest. By the way, the odds of it getting back to him are pretty good; it's so unusual for a wife to respect her husband in that way that people almost invariably talk about it.

ORAL SEX—THREE THOUSAND MILES AWAY

If you live in a larger city, go pick up your local newspaper and you may find (depending on your state laws) dozens of ads for "phone sex"—1-900 numbers where men actually pay three dollars or more *a minute* to hear a woman talk filthy to them.

No doubt about it, this is perverted stuff. But for this industry to thrive like it has, there must be something behind it. I've never called one of these lines, although I've been tempted to from a psychological perspective just to see what they're about. The first time I heard about them, I just couldn't believe a man would pay that much money for what seems like such a silly service.

But you know what these purveyors of phone pornography have discovered? The power of words. When a woman says something a man can visualize, those vivid words can bring him all the way to orgasm. I guarantee you, those men aren't calling for casual conversation. If there wasn't a payoff, so to speak, they wouldn't be paying so much money.

What are these women really saying (in a false, sick way)? "I want you." "I need you." "If I was with you right now, you could do anything you want." I'm sure it's as vulgar as it gets, yet it's a thriving, multimillion-dollar business.

You know what kind of husbands are calling? The kind who get a steady dose of "not now, not here, you'll wake the children, is that all you ever think about?"

Have you ever thought of using "creative" language with your husband? We'll talk about this more in a later chapter, but I want to plant the idea in your mind right now.

"But Dr. Leman! You don't want me to talk like a phone-sex worker, do you?"

Not exactly, but consider this: Imagine a fifteen-year-old girl having a baby. It's kind of a sad thought, isn't it? You know the father probably won't be around, and there isn't a fifteen-year-old on this planet who is mature enough to really care for a child on her own.

Now imagine a twenty-five-year-old who has been married for three years giving birth. You think of the happy grand-parents, the fixed-up nursery, the joy on that couple's face.

The same event is taking place—the birth of a child—but one is very right and the other feels very wrong.

Sex play can be like that. I'm not asking you to be lewd, crude, and offensive. But I want you to understand that the words you use in bed are more than listened to; they are sa-vored, studied, and memorized. If you throw out a phrase or two that seems totally out of character outside the bed-room, you may be surprised at how thrilling it is to your hus-band inside the bedroom.

JUST BECAUSE IT'S CRUDE DOESN'T MEAN IT'S NOT REAL

Many a woman has heard the crass phrase "lover's nuts." In dating relationships, boyfriends will often try to pressure young women to engage in sexual relations by talking about how much it hurts to abstain. You already know what I think about that.

But in a marital situation, wives need to understand that there's some truth to that phrase. Some days a guy will wake up in a state of full erection. He may approach his wife and be refused, but that refusal will do nothing to diminish his desire.

How do I put this in a way that won't offend some of the more sensitive readers? Let me put it this way: It really *can* hurt! Your husband isn't lying to you. There are times when sexual release feels very much like an urgent need to a man. I'll be honest with you: If there's anything worse than this sensation, I haven't discovered it. (Except, perhaps, getting kicked there.)

Women need to understand that if a guy gets frisky, she can quickly dismiss him by saying, "Oh, you're always frisky," and totally put it out of her mind. But the man is still literally hurting. The gun is loaded, the last bullet has been put in the chamber, the target has been sighted in, and the trigger is just moving back. So to be casually tossed aside when you're so close is terribly frustrating.

"I'd never tease my husband and then pull back," some wives might say, but I'm not talking about that. Sometimes a husband *wakes up this way*. Sometimes he comes home from work and sees his wife getting undressed and feels this way. You may not realize how far along he really is on the scale of arousal because your body works so differently—but he feels like he's practically dying to get intimate.

What does this have to do with you? Those quickies and hand jobs we've talked about can be a very practical and very loving thing for a wife to do. Your husband isn't trying to sell you a bill of goods. He's asking you to help him out; you can go a long way toward making him feel loved by responding generously.

BECOMING MORE SEXUAL

Too many of my female clients assume that sexual interest is either there or it isn't. They assume that the presence of arousal is something that has its own mind. It comes and it goes; there's nothing they can do to increase it or maintain it.

This simply isn't true. You may not naturally think of sex as often as your husband would like you to, but—out of love for your husband—you can cultivate a greater interest in sex, and I encourage you to do that.

Dr. Douglas Rosenau has a wonderful list of ten things you can do to "keep lovemaking on the front burner of your marriage."[21]

1. Budget in and spend a certain amount of money each month on your sex life, such as lingerie, new sheets, and nights or weekends away together.
2. Every now and then wear a sexy piece of lingerie all day and allow its unusual feel to remind you of sex constantly.
3. Don't wear any underwear to a social gathering, and tell your husband on the way out the door. You will drive him crazy while you keep aroused.
4. Plan a sexual surprise at least once a month in which you try to blindside your husband in an arousing sexual way.
5. Keep a mental note, and regardless of fatigue or low interest, initiate sex at least once a week.
6. Have fun with your husband's visual arousal, and flaunt your nude body at unusual times just to enjoy his reactions.
7. Take a bubble bath and indulge in other sensual delights at the end of a tiring day—it's a great aphrodisiac and tunes you in to your body.
8. Create romantic sexual fantasies about your love life while driving in the car, and share them with your mate at the end of your day.
9. Use a special perfume that you have associated in your mind with making love, and wear it on the evening or the day you anticipate sexual activity.
10. Practice Kegel exercises (we discuss this on page 98–99).

[21]Dr. Douglas Rosenau, *A Celebration of Sex* (Nashville: Thomas Nelson, 1994), 193.

If you wanted your husband to converse more and he simply said, "Sorry, talk just doesn't interest me as much as it interests you," you'd be hurt, wouldn't you? In fact, some of you probably have husbands who have said something very similar. Or if your husband was habitually lazy, refusing to help, saying that working around the house held little interest for him, you'd soon grow weary of his disinterest and want him to change, wouldn't you?

When you tell your husband you just don't have any interest in sex, you're doing the same thing. In fact, what you're doing is *worse*. You can always call up a girlfriend to talk or hire a handyman to work around the house, but your husband has no place else to go to express sexual intimacy.

Sexual interest can be cultivated and maintained. You may need to make some conscious changes, but it can happen—and if that's what's needed for you to love your husband better, that's what *should* happen.

DEAD SALMON

Another issue that frequently comes up in the counseling room concerns what happens after sex. As a young husband, I was shocked to learn that when the deed was done, Sande wanted me to caress her hands and keep stroking her arms for a half hour or more. When talking to men, I try to stress to them the importance of after-sex attention, but let me be an advocate for the men now that I'm talking to women.

I have a friend who lives in the Pacific Northwest. Every December or January, he and his family usually hike up the Nooksack River to watch the bald eagles. These large birds gather by the dozens, sometimes with as many as eight or nine eagles sitting in a single tree.

What brings those bald eagles to the Pacific Northwest? Dead and dying salmon. You know those fish you pay four or five or seven dollars a pound for in the supermarket? In

December and January, you could practically walk across the Nooksack River on the backs of dead salmon. Once they spawn, they roll over and die.

After a man has had sex, he feels like that salmon. It's a biological reality—we flop over to our side and gasp for our last breath as we usually slip off to sleep. It may seem uncaring to you, but we don't mean it that way. We have to consciously fight not to slip right off into deep relaxation or sleep.

Please try to be understanding here. Your husband is thinking, *Lady, I just gave you all the attention I have and then some, and you want more?* Caring husbands will try to overcome this but, at times, all of us will succumb to the "great sleep."

So the choice is yours: By your willingness, attitude, and words, you can make your husband feel like the luckiest man on the face of the planet; or, by your repeated denials, cutting remarks, and resentment, you can emasculate him and make him feel miserable. That's a lot of power! But our Creator must have felt you could handle this power since he designed men and women this way. If God were to measure your kindness and generosity solely by how well you treat your husband in this area, what do you think he would say?

10

Thirty-One Flavors—
and None of Them Are Ice Cream!

*S*ande and I have been going to Caruso's, a restaurant here in Tucson, for almost forty years now. Yet all I've ever had there is the lasagna.

It drives Sande crazy.

"Why don't you get the chicken cacciatore?" she asked me once.

"'Cause I don't like the chicken cacciatore!"

"But if you got the chicken cacciatore, I could have a bite."

"Listen, honey, if you want a bite of the chicken cacciatore, I'll order you the chicken cacciatore."

"But then I can't have the chicken Giovanni! You always get lasagna here!"

Lasagna does it for me. Why take a chance?

But here's the deal: As much as I love lasagna, I don't want to eat it every night. Once a week, maybe. Twice a week? Probably not. As much as I love that tender pasta, gooey cheese, and zippy tomato sauce, I could only take so much.

ARRANGE SOME LITTLE SURPRISES . . .

You're probably already ahead of where I'm going. The missionary position is a wonderful way to align two bodies. I can't think of a better one. It's intimate, tender, and the results have been proven over generations. Probably three-quarters of the world has been conceived through it, and who knows how many mind-blowing orgasms have resulted from it?

But if you're going to make love twice a week or more, even the missionary position is going to get a little stale. In this chapter, we're going to experiment a little bit. Be forewarned: An exercise or two might offend some of you, but that's okay. If something doesn't get your motor running, don't take that exit. Pass on by to the next one.

But if your spouse is intrigued, maybe, on a special night, you could arrange a little surprise. . . .

Barely Covered

"Why should I drop fifty dollars on new lingerie? He never lets me wear it for more than five minutes!"

Marcia's complaint makes sense—to a woman. But any man could tell you that those five minutes are pretty special. The truth is, most men want their wives to come to bed with clothes on rather than be nude.

Why, you may ask?

So we can take them off.

I'm a firm believer in monogamy—two people who for their entire lives never share sexual relations with anyone other than their spouse. But let's face it: People like variety. Lingerie sets the stage for variety. Different men like different styles. Some like lace, some like see-through; some like satin, some like leather; some like vivid colors; most probably like black. Your choice of lingerie can set the mood—classic, "naughty," Victorian. Switch it around, keep your man guessing, and you'll keep him happy.

Another thing that wearing lingerie will do for your husband is signal that you've thought about this sexual encounter before it took place—and that will really thrill him. He'll realize you decided to go to a store that sells lingerie. You looked through the racks. You purchased something you thought he'd like, and then you planned an evening to show it to him. What I wouldn't give for a camera that would show you how that makes a man feel inside. If you could see his reaction, you'd do it all the time. The people at your local lingerie store would know you by your first name.

Light My Fire
This might sound cheesy to some of you, but try it and see. Stores like Target and Wal-Mart usually carry GE stained-glass bulbs that cast a different light in the bedroom. These can be fun for special occasions.

In my opinion, the best way to vary lighting is with candles; the number and even color of the candles can affect the ambience. At any rate, what you're doing is changing the location—or at least the appearance of the location—in which you make love. Doing so for less than five dollars isn't a bad deal.

Scent-sational!
Scent is another way to keep things new and fresh in bed. So women, try a new perfume. Use a new bath gel. Your goal is that as soon as you climb into bed, your husband's nose will be pleasantly hit with something he's never smelled before. That'll make him come alive in ways that might surprise you.

Men, just for fun, you might like to know that researchers have actually studied what smells are most attractive to women. "Researchers at the Smell and Taste Treatment and Research Foundation in Chicago . . . found that a combination of black licorice candy, cucumber, baby powder, lavender and pumpkin pie caused the greatest increase in female sexual arousal. Black licorice plus cucumber was the most arousing scent; cherry was the most inhibiting. . . . The researchers found that men's cologne actually reduced arousal levels."[22] Cucumber . . .?? Oh, well, they're the researchers.

In other words, guys, cut up a cucumber salad, sprinkle some baby powder on your chest, eat a piece of pumpkin pie and one stick of black licorice, shoot some lavender air freshener in the room, and your wife will be good to go!

Here's a clever suggestion for the women: Tell your husband you've "hidden" your perfume somewhere on your body, and you want him to go find it. He'll enjoy the search as much as you do!

Switch the Sheets

Men, here's a good way to really treat your wife. Linen, cotton, and silk sheets all have their own feel. Since women enjoy the sensual aspect of sex so much, it can be a real treat to surprise them with a new set of sheets. Sheets touch more of your spouse's body than you ever can, so new sheets can really make a difference in how lovemaking feels.

But men—catch a clue. Giving your wife a new set of sheets that are still wrapped up isn't a particularly sexy thing to do. Change the bed yourself and surprise her when you pull back the covers.

The type of sheets you choose can help set the pace for your lovemaking. Cotton might be the comfortable choice for long, slow sex. Silk might heat up the intensity. And if you really want to get wild, consider using a plastic sheet cover (or a shower curtain) and a bottle of baby oil—that's an entirely new sensation!

Another thing that men can do besides get entirely new sheets is to put something on the sheets. I stayed at a hotel

---

[22]Dr. Judith Reichman, *I'm Not In the Mood* (New York: William Morrow and Company, 1998), 136.

room once and noticed when I pulled back the covers that right behind the headboard, on the carpeted floor, was about a dozen roses' worth of petals. Some thoughtful husband must have created a bed of rose petals for his wife on a previous trip. What a wonderful idea.

Any soft flower will do—just pull off the petals and strew them all over the bed. They'll create a new sensation as you lie down on them, and you can also use them to caress your partner. You might want to grab up a handful and sprinkle them on your spouse before sliding on top of her. The smell and feel will provide a new and very pleasurable experience.

The Daring Do

The young wife picked up her tired husband from the airport and started driving down the freeway. "I'm eager for you to see my new haircut," she said.

"I'm sorry," he apologized. "I didn't notice it."

"Of course not," she teased. "I'm not talking about my head."

Whoa, Nelly! She had his attention!

You may be wary of close shaving "down there," as it can be uncomfortable, but some women use depilatories, which means no itching when the hair grows back. A simple trim can also work wonders.

Think about it: You spend hundreds or even thousands of dollars a year to groom the hair on your head, and many of you spend at least thirty minutes a day re-grooming that hair before you go out of the house. How about providing your husband with a special treat by grooming some of the other hair that grows on your body?

The discomfort issue (especially as the hair grows back) will probably keep most wives from doing this as a style of life—but on those special occasions, wow! Remember: For your man, new is almost always more exciting.

Sex Ends *in the Kitchen!*

Many of you may be familiar with my book *Sex Begins in the Kitchen*, in which I talk about how a husband needs to see helping out with the dishes as foreplay—but why reserve the kitchen for foreplay alone? If the kids are gone, you can have a four-course, sexual gourmet experience in the kitchen!

Get creative. That rolling pin, if used lightly, can offer a refreshing massage. The powdered sugar sifter can be used to dust more than pastry—creating a "sweet" sexual experience for both partners. Ordinary straws can become tantalizing treats in the hands of a creative spouse. Lightly blowing focused air on various parts of your lover's body creates wonderful sensations.

Look in the refrigerator/freezer. See those ice cubes? Find some creative ways to make them melt. And that leftover frosting . . . Hmmm. Now what could we do with that? Oh, look—there's some chocolate sauce, and honey, maybe even some whipped cream.

Why haven't you used this room before?

Light-ning!

Okay, picture this. The room is completely dark. You're both under the covers, as naked as you'll ever be, except for your wedding bands. Suddenly your spouse pulls out a small penlight and begins exploring your body. The dark makes it look almost new; the light points out pleasant areas he or she may never have appreciated before—at least, not like this!

Appropriately Playful

Women, if you've got a piece of underwear that is getting ready to be thrown away, don't toss them in the garbage. Instead, shock your husband by standing in front of him wearing just that piece of clothing and saying, "If you can get these off me, I'm all yours."

Resist a little bit, but not too much. You might even dangle a pair of scissors in front of him.

I know, it might seem silly that your husband would like to cut your underwear off you, but a vast majority of them will find this to be an exciting turn-on.

Trust me.

Mirror, Mirror, on the Wall

There's a luxurious hotel, The Garden Suite, in Buffalo, New York, that has learned how to keep the romance alive in many a marriage. One of the deluxe rooms has a private Jacuzzi tub that's plenty big for two people, but a big Jacuzzi isn't all that special. What makes this a little different are the two wall-sized mirrors on each side of it.

Look, ladies, your husband is turned on by sight. I'm not talking about centerfolds here. I think porn can destroy a marriage. You don't have to look like Pamela Anderson to attract your husband. He wants to see *you*.

Here's the trick: Looking at you in a mirror creates an entirely new sensation. Wow, will he love it!

Let him undress you—in front of a mirror. If you need to have the lights dimmed so you don't feel too conspicuous, so be it. Maybe you can use candlelight instead. But allow your husband to become enthralled with your body. You don't want him to look at *Playboy* or go to strip clubs—and if he's a loving husband, he won't do either—but let him look at you.

If you really want to be adventurous, let him make love to you in front of a mirror. Let him fill his eyes. When you do that, you create even more desire for yourself in him. You fill his heart, and he'll feel unusually close to you as a result.

Unless you have a movable mirror nearby, you may need to check out a hotel room to find one that will work. Something across the room will seem too far away (like you're looking into the wrong end of a telescope) and completely spoil the effect. If you or your husband has to squint to get a glimpse of what's happening, you're defeating the purpose.

Consider pulling up a comforter or a soft blanket right next to a mirror. If you can find a place where there are mirrors on two different walls, you can increase the effect. For some people, watching what they're doing will be unusually stimulating; it's something I think every couple should probably try at least once.

Afternoon Delight

I've read the entire Bible. Not once does it say you have to wait until it gets dark to have sex. So many married couples—particularly those with kids—fall into the trap of waiting until everything else is done before they can even think about having sex. The kids have to be in bed, the carpets need to be vacuumed, the dinner dishes need to be washed and put away, etc. Then, and only then, is sex even considered. Unfortunately, by this time, one or both spouses are likely to be sleeping.

What couple hasn't faced this dilemma? You wake up thinking about sex and may even engage in a little light foreplay. Maybe you're rushed—you have to get to work or you need to get the kids up in time to catch the bus—so you promise each other that passion is going to fly like a jet fighter plane later that night. Throughout the morning, both of you think about what you're going to do to each other later on; in the afternoon, you imagine how everything is going to feel. By 6:00 P.M., you're feeling rushed. Dinner isn't on the table yet, and Melody is lagging behind on her homework. Finally, at 7:05, you've got some semblance of food in front of the family. By 8:30, everyone is fed and the dishes are halfway done.

Meanwhile Joshua started the bathtub, went in search of his favorite toy, and forgot about the running water until his younger sister screamed that there was a river coming out under the bathroom door. Older sister Melody is asking for more help with that math homework. And both of you are dog-tired.

By 10:30, the last child is finally in bed, and sex suddenly seems like an obligation more than a delight. How could something that sounded so wonderful just ten hours ago now sound like more work?

Don't let sex become the last in a long list of things to do.

Physiologically, a man's body is most ready to engage in sex first thing in the morning. Most business-affair trysts are carried out during the lunch hour. And many dating couples find that when they make a dinner date, dinner is the last thing on their minds. So why is it that only married couples seem to put off sex until last in the day?

I know, I know—you're too busy. We'll talk about that more in a later chapter. If you have the resources, get a baby-sitter, reserve a room at a local hotel, and enjoy the marriage-saving potential of hotel sex, right in the middle of the day. You've got a clean bed, and you don't have to make it when you leave. It may not be cheap, but divorce is even more expensive in the long run.

Keep Your Spouse Guessing

One of the biggest complaints I hear from wives is that their husbands seem to be following some predetermined road map: "He kisses me three times, spends ninety seconds kissing and caressing my right nipple, thirty seconds on my left, puts his hand between my legs for three minutes, and then he's inside me."

For both men and women, one of the keys to sexual fulfillment is to keep your spouse guessing. One wife I counseled was very compliant, but pretty unimaginative. She was always willing, but her husband wanted more than willing—he wanted aggressive. One night, she just about rocked his world. He was on top of her, going through foreplay when all of a sudden, she took over, pushing him on his back, acting like she was in a rush, like she couldn't wait for penetration. Then she climbed on top of him and went at it with enthusiasm, like she *needed* it. He was one of the happiest husbands I've ever seen as he described what happened.

The main thing is to keep your spouse guessing. You can't do this every week of course, or maybe even every month—but from time to time it's vital that you truly surprise your spouse. Let her wonder what's coming next. If you're one of those guys who always starts "upstairs," then goes "downstairs," surprise her! Start by spending five minutes *caressing her feet,* maybe rubbing in some lotion, maybe even kissing them, and then work your way up from there. Or maybe have her lie on her stomach and find some things to do on her back.

If you're a woman who normally dresses conservatively, why not buy a dress that you'd *never* wear in public—but put it on to greet your husband when he comes home? Or consider making him strip naked while you stay clothed!

Noise, Noise, Noise

Silence isn't golden—at least, not in the bedroom. Husbands, when you murmur or voice your approval, your wife feels wonderful. Everyone wants to be good in bed, but your wife may not know how good she is making you feel unless you tell her.

Wives, up your vocal activities by twofold or even threefold. A lot of women don't realize they can bring a man to orgasm by simply saying the right words. Remember: A wife's sexual enthusiasm is the number one turn-on for men. The louder you are, the more we love it. Use words, moans, murmurs, purring, even grunts or screams. Your husband will love it.

The most intimate noise, of course, is to hear your own name spoken in the throes of passion—perhaps the biggest turn-on there is. Say your spouse's name. Instead of, "You turn me on," say, "You turn me on, Robert. I can't believe how much I want you." Or men could say, "Oh, Andrea, you're so beautiful. I love the way you feel."

If sexy talk is hard for you, try this: Use a blindfold the next time you make love. Taking away the visual may help you emphasize the vocal. Describe what you're doing or want done—communicate only through words so that, in time, "verbal caressing" becomes a natural part of love play.

I already know what some of you are thinking: *But Dr. Leman, we have kids sleeping in the next room!*

Not having to worry about noise is one of the delights of hotel sex. But even when you're home, you can help soundproof your room by turning on a noisy fan, air conditioner, or putting on some light music. You might also consider soundproofing your bedroom. There are options that aren't as expensive as you might think, and if it makes you feel less inhibited in the bedroom, it's a worthy investment.

In the meantime, if you whisper something very erotic right into your husband's ear, there's not a chance your kids will hear it—or your husband will ever forget it!

Leave Me Breathless

Want to give your partner a special treat? The next time you're kissing her breasts, back away just enough so you can blow on them with your breath. If you're close, your breath will feel hot. Now back away a few more inches and blow gently—this will make your breath feel cold. It's a delightful sensation.

Women, you can also do this to the man's penis during oral sex. But men, you need to be careful—blowing into your wife's vagina when she's pregnant is dangerous.

SEXUAL PLAY

In this section, I want to look at the lighter side of sex. While I believe sex is a very meaningful and very spiritual act, let's face it–it can also be a lot of fun! Here are just a few ideas to pair laughter and sex.

Concentration

If you're up for a lighter form of sex, try this: One spouse picks a challenge while the two of you are lying in bed. An example might be, "I bet I can name more states that begin with the letter *M* than you can."

At first glance this game sounds simple and boring, but I've left out a few details. First, neither of you is wearing any clothes. Second, the spouse who asks the question is completely free to do *whatever* he or she wants to the other spouse's body in order to "distract" them. Licking is allowed. So is kissing, blowing hot air, or other creative distractions.

Strip Foosball

Some preteen boy would probably be grossed out and mortified if he knew how much his parents were enjoying his favorite Christmas gift. You see, one night the wife decided to challenge her TV-watching husband to a game. He wasn't all that interested until she said, "How about if the loser of each point has to take off an item of clothing?"

Her husband was on that game in less than three seconds flat. The wife was surprised–her husband had seen her naked who knows how many times, but there's still something exciting about seeing it happen piece by precious piece.

Maybe you don't have a foosball table. How about using a child's puzzle, a simple game, or the old-fashioned deck of cards (strip poker)? You don't like the idea of strip poker? Okay, then, how about strip go-fish?

Food and Sex

"So," I ask the young man, enjoying watching him squirm. "What restaurant are you taking my daughter to?"

"Joe's Oyster Bar," he replies.

"That's a seafood restaurant, isn't it?" I ask. Suddenly the temperature in the room is gaining about ten degrees a minute. Joe's is famous—obviously—for its oysters. And oysters are known to be an aphrodisiac—just the kind of dinner that's designed to lower a young woman's natural inhibitions.

"Yes it is," he says, a rivulet of sweat dropping from his forehead and diving down his nose.

"Pretty crowded there on a Friday night, don't you think?"

"I have reservations, sir."

"Reservations? So you planned this in advance, huh?"

"I guess so. I thought your daughter . . ."

"You know, Bob's Burger Bar is cheaper. My daughter loves a good burger."

"Yessir, I was just thinking that maybe we should go a little casual tonight. I'll cancel the reservation."

"Well, look at this—I just happen to have a phone right here. . . ."

This young man and I both knew what was really being discussed. Oysters, green M&Ms, strawberries with whipped cream, you name it—somebody has probably tried to ascribe the powers of an aphrodisiac to it. While the science behind this connection is often lacking, sex is just as much mental as physical. So if you think a food is sexy and a turn-on, it *becomes* an aphrodisiac.

Joining food and sex is a popular way to enjoy two favorite pastimes. As a couple of women writers note: "A number of women told us that they find sharing chocolate with their partner to be especially erotic: chocolate in a hot tub, chocolate with champagne, chocolate in bed. If you think your partner may tend toward that particular pleasure, keep a box of special chocolates within easy reach."[23]

While it would go beyond science to call chocolate a bona

---

[23]Sanna with Miller, *How to Romance*, 86.

fide aphrodisiac, it's true that chocolate raises the level of serotonin in your brain, which, while stopping short of directly affecting your libido, does tend to promote a happy and warm feeling.

If you want to test this out, you might want to pay a visit to The Spa at the Hotel Hershey in Hershey, Pennsylvania. They actually have a chocolate-soak recipe that they offer to their guests. You can order the "Whipped Cocoa Bath" direct from The Hershey Spa[24] or create your own version by adding three tablespoons of cocoa powder, one tablespoon of powdered milk, lots of hot water, a bathtub you don't mind getting a little dirty, and two naked bodies. Some people like to add whipped cream to their "hot chocolate"—where the cream is *applied* is entirely up to you.

You can also use food to set the mood by making it an invitation. There isn't a man on this planet who wouldn't know what his wife was thinking if he opened his briefcase and found a baggie of green M&Ms with a note that said, "Eat lots of these and come home right after work!" Most wives would catch on pretty quickly if their husbands walked into the bedroom with some strawberries and whipped cream.

Of course, it's not just *what* you eat that can set the mood but *how* you eat. Reduced lighting can be a wonderfully seductive experience. If the kids are gone, or you're eating in your hotel room, dim the lights and eat in the nude! One wife gave her husband a real treat by calling him on his cell phone, just when she knew he'd be in the worst part of his commute.

"Honey, I've got some bad news," she said.

"What's that?"

"It's been a hectic day, so there isn't a clean plate in the house. That gives us two choices."

"What are they?"

[24]The Spa at the Hotel Hershey, 1-717-520-5888 or www.spaathotelhershey.com.

"Well, we could eat out, or you could hurry home and use my naked stomach as a plate."

Let me tell you, that guy got home in record time!

Whether clothed or not, feeding each other is a pretty sensuous experience, as is both of you eating off just one plate. There's something very intimate about sharing just one setting. You have to sit very close, and the process of putting food in your spouse's mouth is a powerful act of intimacy that can set off all sorts of delicious and even animalistic passions.

A guy I worked with told me about the time he took his wife to a restaurant in San Francisco that caters to people who want to eat leisurely dinners. There's no rush, the booths are somewhat isolated, and the atmosphere is more than a little romantic. I remember him telling me about how he was feeding his wife, putting food very gently into her mouth, when she shocked him by saying, "Put your finger in my mouth next time."

"So what?" I said.

"Kevin, you have no idea what a turn-on that was."

There *is* something sensual about eating.

FREQUENTLY ASKED QUESTIONS

While I'm a big fan of variety, it's certainly true that couples can carry some things too far. The Bible is amazingly free in what it allows and even encourages a married couple to do in bed—but modern technology has provided some options about which many couples are understandably wary. Here are some of the most frequently asked questions in that regard.

What about the use of sexual "toys," including vibrators?
There is nothing in the Bible that prohibits the use of such marital enhancers, provided that nothing is degrading to, or unwanted by, either partner. As a way to provide variety within the marriage, the occasional use of toys can be a very

good idea. In general, however, most women will find such orgasms less emotionally satisfying than the kind that result from body-to-body contact. Speaking as a psychologist, I think you'll find that such aids are occasionally fun, but not the kind of thing that builds lasting intimacy.

What about anal sex?

I'm surprised at the frequency with which this question arises. I don't know where men are getting the idea, but increasingly, even among Christian couples, this is becoming an issue, typically with the husband desiring it and asking for it and the wife showing strong reluctance.

I think part of the allure is that, for some men, anal sex seems "naughty," and they think it might spice up their marriage. However, God designed the vagina to receive a penis; it was custom-made to engage in intercourse. The anus, quite frankly, was not. Anal sex will hurt. Yes, some women stretch out that area to gradually accommodate a husband, but there are other issues, hygienic and otherwise, that bring this practice into question. A woman's rectal area can easily tear, resulting in painful and embarrassing maladies—and how will she explain this to a doctor? And when you throw in the issue of hemorrhoids (which 70 percent of people will experience at some point in their life) and the like, it's best to leave this practice alone. Did I say all that too nicely? If I did, I apologize. It's kinky, and I believe it's wrong!

This is one area where I tell men they need to let go of this expectation or fantasy. It's reasonable and understandable for a wife to say, "I want to experiment and keep variety in our lovemaking, but this is something I just don't want to do."

What about couples using pornographic movies together?

One of the things we know about addictions today—and we've learned a lot about them—is that one of the most powerful addictions known to humankind is the addiction to pornography. The vast majority of people who rent pornography are men but, eventually, many couples decide to rent a racy video just to "spice things up."

I think this is a very dangerous act. For starters, why can't a husband just be satisfied with you? Why would a man want to look at other naked women? I'm a man with a high libido, but I don't need anything but Sande to get me aroused. In fact, I can get sexually excited watching my fifty-plus wife fill the dishwasher!

Secondly, speaking as a psychologist, watching pornography together can be a slippery slope. If you're married to a man who has the mind-set "anything goes, including all the sleaze, if it gets us hot," you're eventually going to get into some very questionable practices. Why? Because pornography is usually addictive to men. It probably won't be addictive to you women, but you're not the ones I'm worried about. A number of wives have confessed that watching pornography does tend to put them "in the mood," but I ask them, overall and *long-term*, is this good for your marriage or harmful for your marriage? Here's a clue: Watching porn won't make your husband treat you better, encourage him to spend more time with the kids, or be more helpful around the house . . . the very things that make most wives desire their husbands more.

One of my little theories about raising kids is that you shouldn't start habits you don't want to have to continue throughout your child's graduate-school education. This is one habit that will become ever more demanding and probably demented.

Added to this is the natural experience that the wife will eventually begin comparing herself to the women in the movie or on the pages of the magazines. It's only human for her to do this. In that situation, just how loved and cherished does a woman feel? Does she feel adored, or is she secretly wondering, *When his eyes were closed was he fantasizing about doing it with* her?

Another thing that really troubles me about pornography is the industry you're supporting by purchasing it. Think about it: Focus on the Family isn't putting this stuff out! You're supporting people who generally are hostile to religion and faith and family. They make their money by exploiting young women, and they entice many men into lifelong addictions. The fact is, those actors are adulterers! In my book, these are not the type of people I want to give my dollars to.

Most clean couples who get into this eventually sense what I call the "Uh-oh" phenomenon—that inner agitation signaling that something just isn't right. It's best to pay close attention to that uneasiness, because it's usually our conscience trying to protect us.

TOO MUCH IS TOO MUCH

Married sexuality provides a solid foundation for peak sexual intimacy. Because the two of you are committed to each other until death separates you, you're never on trial. You need have no fear if a "great idea" for sexual fun bombs. You don't have to worry about one or the other leaving if, during a particular season, sexual intensity cools down a bit.

You also don't need to apologize if you just want plain old missionary-position sex more often than not. It's unrealistic to expect that every sexual experience is going to provide mind-blowing orgasms that send you to the moon and back. Sexual intimacy is built around playful times of love; long, slow, and sensual times of love; exciting and adventurous love; and quick, passionate love.

Please don't feel that you have to have variety *every time* you hop into bed together. There's a reason you have some favorite positions—you like them! Enjoy routine sex, exciting sex, fast sex, slow sex, and unexpected sex. Take it all, appreciate it all, and let it create the intimacy between you and your spouse that God designed it to build.

11

Turning Off the Turnoffs

*M*y first cigarette was a Viceroy, smoked on the handlebars of Eddie Schutts's bike, when I was just seven years old. I was about four feet high at the time, but I felt taller than Wilt Chamberlain with that white stick hanging out of my lips.

That one incident started a fourteen-year habit that picked up steam when I turned twelve. During the summers, passing motorists often chucked cigarette butts out their car windows, thinking all the life had been sucked out of the cigarettes. How little they knew. My friends and I raced over and picked them up, stealing a few quick puffs until there wasn't a shred of tobacco left.

I also "recycled" my dad's Lucky Strikes. It was my job to clean out the ashtrays at home, which I gladly did, sticking the bigger leftovers in my pocket for later consumption. Those

Lucky Strikes were strong suckers—they went straight to the lungs.

Recently someone asked me when I quit smoking and why. Had I read the attorney general's report and warning?

Nah. I'm so old they didn't have warnings back then.

Did I get concerned about lung damage?

Nope.

Was it the expense?

Are you kidding me? Back in my day, packs cost just twenty cents. That was before the government discovered cigarette taxes could become a veritable money machine.

Did I hate the taste?

Au contraire! Even today, three decades after I quit, I can still remember how good a cigarette tasted after a meal.

So what made me quit?

I fell in love with a beautiful woman named Sande. From our early conversations, I learned that Sande went to church.

Uh-oh, I thought. *Smoking might be a problem.*

The "might" was removed when Sande smelled me at the start of a date. "Eeewww!" she said. "You've been smoking!"

It was a playful challenge, but I was crazy about this girl and didn't want to take any chances. So that, my friends, was the last cigarette I ever smoked. Don't get me wrong: I loved my Salems, but I loved Sande even more.

The nicotine addiction was real—psychologically and physically. But for the sake of my relationship with Sande, I was willing to turn my back on my little white friends. I wasn't going to let a past history or habit steal my future.

That's the key right there: Are you going to let a past history or habit steal your future?

We've already talked about your sexual past, but in this chapter, we're going to look at how you can turn off those things that turn you off from sex. If sex is as important to a marriage as I believe it is, it's vital that you learn how to be less encumbered in bed. You are not a slave to thought patterns that steal sexual freedom; you can fight back.

Here's how.

PARENTAL INHIBITIONS

One of my first jobs as a counselor when I'm working with newly married couples is getting them to cut the apron strings from Mom and Dad. You have to leave before you cleave, and women in particular can have a difficult time doing this. Sometimes the couple will bring up a sexual inhibition the wife has, and when we explore why this is an issue, she will say, "But what if my mom or dad knew I was doing that? They'd be disgusted!"

How do you know? When Sande and I gave birth to our youngest child at the respective ages of forty-seven and forty-nine, our oldest kids' first thought was, *Eeewwww. You mean you guys still do it?* They knew we must have had sex on at least five different occasions (since we have five children), and then they figured that maybe there had been another five times when we decided to celebrate an anniversary, for a total of ten times. If only they knew that number is close to our weekly record!

While it may not be appropriate for you to discuss specific sexual activities with your parents, you really don't know if they would be offended. Take it from an old geezer: It just might be that your parents have *perfected* that one little practice you think would mortify them even to mention.

Secondly, even if you did know it would bother them, *so what?!* It's time to cut the apron strings. Just because your parents wanted to settle for less, why should you? It's time to turn off that turnoff!

Some readers may have grown up in environments that were hyper-Victorian. They got the early message in life that sex is wrong, dirty, terrible, and disgusting. And you know what? Sex *can* be exactly that, particularly outside of marriage.

But it wasn't designed to be that way. Within the protective, covering bonds of marriage, sex is a great and wonderful gift. Unfortunately, that knowledge doesn't always help a woman who has had it drilled into her head from the time she was little that sex was something to avoid.

Footnote to every parent: What are you communicating to your sons and daughters about sex? I hope it's not that sex is bad, because, quite frankly, the day will come when your kids discover otherwise. You'll have put yourself in a very bad place because from that day on, your kids will think, *Mom and Dad don't have a clue!*

When I'm talking to a couple where the woman is from a hyper-Victorian background, I start by talking to the husband. He has to get behind his wife's eyes and understand how fearful she is of sex. This part is not an option: He *must* become an extremely gentle and patient lover. He needs to learn to accept the small offerings his wife is able to give him, and focus with gratitude on what she *is* doing rather than obsess about what she *won't* do.

Then I talk to the wife. If I think she can handle it, I'll say something shocking and blunt so she'll remember it: "Maryanne, the way I see it, you've got two options in front of you: Either *you* will have a love affair with your husband or somebody else will."

Sometimes a statement like that will really make a young woman angry. "How can you say that? If he's going to be like that, I don't want to be married to him anyway!"

Do you see the box she's put her marriage in? Of course I would plead with her husband not to have an affair, but she's casually denying him regular sexual intimacy and then expecting him to be faithful. Most committed men of faith and integrity will rise to the challenge—but a good number of them, unfortunately, won't. Why risk it?

We then talk about a series of small steps the woman can

take to begin loosening up. I usually give her a reading assignment: the Song of Songs. God is very pro-sex, and the Bible is a very descriptive book.

I then ask her to consciously and courageously do some things that might make her uncomfortable. Buy a teddy—and wear it! Make love with candlelight illuminating her body. Take the position on top. Initiate sex.

Through a series of small choices, a woman gradually leaves negative imprinting behind. When she sees how her husband responds, she learns that reaching out sexually is much more fulfilling than shutting down—but her thinking won't change until she starts *doing* things differently.

Fortunately, I've seen scores of women make great progress. It never happens overnight, but if women are faithful to keep making those small choices, eventually they learn that a good sex life is important to their husband and very fun for them!

As one wife told me with a sly smile, "Who knew?" She couldn't believe what she and her husband were doing after ten years of marriage—but now she was enjoying every minute of it.

RELIGIOUS INHIBITIONS

If only you young bucks knew how far our society has come. When I was growing up, no decent, God-fearing woman would say the word *pregnant* in public. If you were a teacher, you were dismissed as soon as you started showing—even if you were married! Ever watch *I Love Lucy* reruns? Notice the single beds?

This is our society and these are our roots; that's the way things were. Religious boards actually got to censor Hollywood movies. Even if you didn't grow up in a society like that, *your mom or dad did,* and they helped pass some of those inhibitions along.

Loretta Lynn, the legendary country singer who is now in her sixties, confesses that, "When I got married, I didn't even know what *pregnant* meant. I was five months pregnant when I went to the doctor and he said, 'You're gonna have a baby.' I said, 'No way. I can't have no baby.' He said, 'Ain't you married?' Yep. He said, 'You sleep with your husband?' Yep. 'You're gonna have a baby, Loretta. Believe me.' And I did."[25]

Our culture has come a long, long way in the past two generations when it comes to being open about sex—further than our grandparents could ever have dreamed. That's had some positive and some negative effects.

While some churches and synagogues have worked hard to address this new sexual openness, many have remained in the 1950s. Just ask yourself this: When was the last time a pastor or rabbi announced an eight-week sermon series on the Song of Songs, or even a *single sermon* on sex? I speak regularly in some of the largest churches in the country, and I almost never hear of a frank discussion about sex taking place on church property. It just doesn't happen. Even in the early days of the twenty-first century, church and sex just aren't seen as two things that go together.

What's funny is that when I bring up the topic in church, thereby giving people permission to discuss sex and ask questions about it, you can't shut them up. They never want to go home. These are the same people who berate the pastor for going three minutes past noon!

I've had a number of women try to use religion as an excuse to avoid becoming sexually available to their husbands. "I don't want any of that far-out stuff," one woman said to me.

"Like what?" I asked.

"Like me being on top. It just isn't natural."

Yes, some people have that narrow a view of sex. They think that sex is for procreation *only*. The majority of people reading this book probably aren't coming from this stand-

[25]Loretta Lynn, interviewed by Andy Ward, "What I've Learned," *Esquire*, January 2002, 62.

point—if you did, you would have stopped reading long before now! But you may be somewhere toward that end of the religious continuum.

Pastor Stephen Schwambach offers some great pastoral advice to those of you who worry that your being sexually expressive within marriage might somehow offend your pastor. He suggests that "you probably have no real knowledge of what your minister would or would not approve. You might be stunned to learn the wide range of sexual freedom he believes the Bible actually permits a husband and wife to enjoy."[26]

What do you expect your pastor to do? Get up in front of the church and read a list of acceptable practices? "Deep french kissing? Wonderful idea. Oral sex—that's okay, too. Doing it with the lights on? Absolutely. After all, God made light, and he made sex—why not join the two together? Whipped cream and strawberries? Well, as long as you're not on Centre Court at Wimbledon, sure, why not?!"

You get the picture. That's not going to happen.

As far as Christianity goes, sexual experience between a husband and a wife is virtually unlimited in its creativity and pleasure. In Judaism, every married woman is granted three fundamental rights: food, clothing, and sexual expression (called *onah*). God tells us in many places not to involve any third person—but two married, consenting adults have a virtual free-for-all in front of them, provided no one is being hurt or degraded and both are acting with sensitivity and love.

You may hear differently, of course. A number of so-called Christian leaders have appointed themselves as the sexual morality patrol for the Christian church. I have no problem when such leaders stick to the Bible, which clearly prohibits prostitution, any sex outside of marriage, homosexuality, and the

[26]Schwambach, *For Lovers Only*, 176.

like. But within marriage, as long as neither partner is getting hurt, biblical prohibitions are virtually silent.

FRIENDLY INHIBITIONS

Some women are held up by the thought of what their girlfriends would say. "Groupthink" can be pretty heavy within the feminine gender: "Oh, Amy, I can't *believe* Bob would even *ask* you to do that! My George would never get that perverted! You poor girl; let me order you a latte."

First off, you have absolutely no business discussing your sexual activities with anyone other than a professional counselor. You want a big turnoff? This may be the biggest one for men. Men consider it an act of infidelity if you talk about sexual matters to others—especially if your talk is to one of his relatives.

Secondly, to women who seem cowed by their friends' approval or disapproval, here's what Schwambach counsels:

> Let's suppose that your girlfriends have compiled a long list of sexual favors that they would never ever be willing to offer to their husbands. Is that something for them to be proud of, or is it a crying, selfish, shortsighted shame?
>
> As a result of their warped sense of feminine "dignity," they are probably married to uptight, unfulfilled men. But your deep love for your husband would never allow him to suffer as their husbands must.
>
> If you have to think such thoughts, go ahead and think them the rest of the way out: "Yes, my girlfriends would give me a hard time if they knew what I am willing to do for my husband. But their husbands would probably give anything if their wives were willing to treat them as well as I enjoy treating my husband!"[27]

[27]Schwambach, *For Lovers Only*, 177.

If you're truly worried about people finding out what the two of you do, *don't tell anyone!* No one has to know! Don't let others who are outside the bedroom steal or detract from the pleasure and intimacy you build inside the bedroom. Kick them out of your bed, and when you're vigorously loving your spouse, kick them out of your mind. Focus solely on giving your spouse the most pleasure you can.

PERSONAL INHIBITIONS

Another big inhibitor of sexual pleasure is embarrassment. Maybe your husband wants you to perform a striptease, or your wife wants you to read poetry or sing to her. Part of you really wants to provide this treat—but you're mortified at the thought of it, and you just can't make yourself do it.

Or at least you *think* you can't. The truth is, when you hold back on something that isn't morally based or personally offensive or degrading, you're stealing from your spouse. When your partner married you, he or she rightfully expected that the two of you would fully enjoy sexual intimacy and pleasure. It's one thing to be embarrassed, but it's another thing entirely to let that embarrassment continue to rob your spouse of sexual fun, spontaneity, and enjoyment.

Schwambach adds, "When you think about it—really think about it . . . you may decide that there is something far more embarrassing than the actions you have rejected up to now. And that is for you to have to explain why you have chosen to deprive your darling of the intimate delights he or she had every right to expect would be his or hers when your mate forsook all others and took you for a lifetime mate."[28]

Sometimes we need to force ourselves to grow, and this may be one of those times for you. The best way to do this is to reconsider that request your spouse made before, the one

[28]Schwambach, *For Lovers Only*, 181.

you thought might even sound fun—making love with the lights on, eating a meal in the nude, whatever it was—but that you turned down out of embarrassment. Now it's your turn to bring it up. You won't believe the smile on your spouse's face when you become the initiator of the very act you once spurned. Your spouse's heart (and more!) will be racing, and he or she will feel very much in love with you for taking this step of courage, intimacy, and love.

Another personal inhibition is a false sense of propriety. Part of this comes from recognizing that the same activity is appropriate and inappropriate in two different places. Some people just never make the change—what they think is inappropriate in public, they never realize can be more than appropriate in private.

I do a lot of seminars and public speaking. When I show up in most churches on Sunday morning, they want me to wear a suit, or at least a coat and a tie. On Saturday afternoon, when I get to watch a football game of my beloved Arizona Wildcats, a suit is the last thing I'm going to wear. I'm more likely to have on an Arizona sweatshirt.

At the different events, I'm also going to act differently. When Arizona scores, I'm going to get out of my seat, scream and yell, and wave my hands. Back at church, I don't take part in a wave after a successful offering, because that type of thing just isn't done. Besides, can't you just imagine beloved Mildred getting faint if the youth group were to start a wave after a record offering or attendance announcement?

Now, is it right or wrong to wear a suit? Depends on where you're going. Is it proper or improper for me to take part in the wave? Depends on where I'm sitting.

The same thing is true for you in bed. No, it's not appropriate for you to throw your breasts—or your cleavage, for that matter—in the face of strangers. But oh, how wonderful it is to entice your husband that way when the two of you are alone: "You want them, honey? They're all yours!"

The problems crop up when a spouse gets hung up on "propriety" in the wrong place. Modesty is not only a good idea—it's commanded in Scripture. The apostle Paul is very clear on this: "I want women to be modest in their appearance. They should wear decent and appropriate clothing and not draw attention to themselves" (1 Timothy 2:9). In other words, don't come to church in a slinky nightgown or a low-plunging dress.

But in the bedroom, propriety means something else altogether! Those breasts that Paul tells you to cover up in public are now to be used to arouse your husband: "A loving doe, a graceful deer. Let her breasts satisfy you always. May you always be captivated by her love" (Proverbs 5:19). According to Keil and Delitzsch, two Old Testament commentators, the Hebrew here is clearly referring to "sensual love." This is hot stuff! These commentators insist that Solomon "speaks here of a morally permissible love-ecstasy . . . , an intensity of love connected with the feeling of superabundant happiness."[29]

Some women and some men, particularly those from very religious homes, occasionally have difficulties making the switch from public propriety to private propriety. Public propriety is essential, but inappropriate "propriety" in private can be deadly to your sex life. Learn to let go, even to stretch the boundaries.

In many ways, Scripture's teaching is this: Don't let anyone besides your spouse enjoy your sexual charms in any way, but then unleash those charms in their full fury upon your husband or wife. Channel all your sexual appeal in one direction. Keep the dam up when others are around; don't let a trickle escape through the walls. But when you're behind closed

[29]C. F. Keil and F. Delitzsch, *Commentary on the Old Testament in Ten Volumes, Vol. VI: Proverbs, Ecclesiastes, Song of Somonom*, Trans. by M. G. Easton (Grand Rapids, Mich.: William B. Eerdmans Publishing Co., reprinted 1973), 130-131.

doors, alone with your spouse, open up the floodgates and let the water flow at full force.

CHOOSING MATURITY

One of the things we've learned about human behavior is that life is a series of choices. Some theorists even suggest mental illness is a choice—you choose to be depressed or not to be depressed. We won't argue those theories here, but there is something to be said for the whole concept of love being primarily a *decision*. Feelings come and go, but the only way they remain is if they are watered and nurtured with thoughts. You have a choice to give yourself to this person fully or, for whatever reason, to hold yourself back. If you hold yourself back, you both lose. Marriage is a voluntary mutual submission to one another. This is a joyous reality when it's lived out unselfishly. It's miserable when one or both partners begin shutting out the other.

Once you've stood up in front of your family and friends and said, "I do," don't turn around at night and say, "I don't." That's what happens in all too many marriages. My hope is that whether your turnoffs have been caused by personal trauma, parental upbringing, a false sense of religion, embarrassment, or anything else, you can make some progress so your sexual life will be everything it can be.

At the very least, be honest. Don't tell yourself, *I can't do that.* Instead admit, "I *won't* do that," or "I don't want to do that." The reality is that you *could* do it, but you're *choosing* not to.

If your spouse is the one with the inhibitions, you can help by being understanding and patient, though firm, in encouraging him or her to seek counseling. Be the type of loving spouse who says, "Honey, we'll get through this together." With both of you working toward that goal of freedom in sexual expression within marriage, maturity will one day be yours. Your tastes will change.

I think back to myself as a seventh-grader. I thought I was so cool sitting in that restaurant with the jukebox playing, eating my glazed doughnut and drinking my root beer in a frosted mug while I smoked my dad's Lucky Strike leftovers. But as I grew up, I found something better. When you're twelve years old, you judge a restaurant by its double cheeseburger, hot fudge sundae, and chocolate milk shakes. Fifteen years later, you might judge a restaurant by its béarnaise sauce.

It's all about maturity. The couple you are today is not the couple you'll be tomorrow. I hope you'll be more loving, more generous, closer to each other, and even freer to express that love in bed.

Sex's Greatest Enemy

I've met few couples who don't desire a fulfilling and meaningful sex life. Even individuals who have lost virtually all sexual interest still, when they're honest, usually *wish* they could get their interest back.

If just about everyone wants to have a better sex life, why do so few of us feel satisfied and content in this area? The greatest enemy of sex is not weight gain. It's not a lack of information. Nor is it financial troubles or having young children around the house. In the wake of Viagra, it's not even impotence!

In fact, the greatest enemy of sex among women is . . .

Weariness.

One women's magazine puts it best:

What's the first thing to go when you're busy, tired, and stressed? If you said sex, you're not alone. An estimated 24 million American women say they don't have time, are too exhausted, or just aren't in the mood for sex, and more than a third of *Redbook* readers say that being too tired is their number one excuse for not having sex. So we put it off for later—but later can easily become never. In case you haven't noticed, abstinence doesn't make the loins grow hotter, it just begets more abstinence.

Sex on the other hand, begets more sex. Studies show that lovemaking elevates the levels of brain chemicals associated with desire. So the best way to increase your yearning for sex is to *have* it.[30]

I have been speaking and writing for years about how the overcommitted pace of American families is killing us socially, relationally, and psychologically. We are simply too busy. Many families I work with could easily cut out 50 percent of their activities and still be tired. That's *not* an exaggeration. Most families who see me are often shocked at the way I can take a meat cleaver to their schedule.

When we live life at the pace of a NASCAR race, sex is one of the first things that goes. Once again, if you want to improve your sex life as a couple, you need to examine your relationship outside the bedroom. What are you doing that is keeping you from sexual intimacy?

Redbook magazine ran a poll on its Web site asking the question, "What would you do with an hour's worth of free time?" Over ten thousand men and women responded. Eighty-five percent of men and 59 percent of women answered *sex*—wide majorities in both cases. Just 12 percent of women chose shopping or extra sleep, followed by watching TV, exercising, reading, and eating.[31]

---

[30]Susan Crain Bakos, "The Sex Trick Busy Couples Swear By," *Redbook*, March 2001, 125.
[31]"You Told Us," *Redbook*, February 2001, 12.

What does this tell you? If you had extra time, the majority of you wouldn't head out to the mall. You wouldn't pick up a book or turn on the television or go to the gym. You'd get naked with your spouse—and your marriages would be much better for it.

How do couples begin to overcome the effects of weariness?

CHANGE YOUR SCHEDULE

There's no use trying to build a beautiful house on a tilted foundation. If you truly want to make your family life and your sexual life more meaningful, you're going to have to give up a few things. No more running around five out of five weekday evenings. I'd say if you're gone more than two evenings a week, something needs to give.

I almost laugh when people ask me, "But won't my kids miss out on a lot of opportunities if I insist we can't be gone more than two evenings a week?" The reason I laugh is because what kids *really* miss is family time. When people come to me for counseling and talk about their childhoods, none of them look back with fond remembrance on a lifestyle that had them out of the house on Monday for Scouts, Tuesday and Thursday for soccer, Wednesday at church, and Friday at a school game. The memories that people cherish are the evenings the entire family stayed at home and played Yahtzee, watched a movie together, or sat around and talked.

Do you and your husband run a family taxi service? "Okay, Jeremy, you've got to leave work early to pick up Wendy from ballet."

"Why?"

"I've got to get Daniel from his tennis lessons. But you'll have to make Wendy leave ballet ten minutes early, because Jennifer needs to get to youth group, and you won't have time if you wait until Wendy's lessons are over. . . ."

Tell me, how can you possibly expect to nurture a loving,

emotionally fulfilling, and close relationship with that kind of dialogue taking place on a regular basis?

Slow down. Mark things off your calendar. Make room for sex.

In fact, let me be blunt: If you're not having sex with your spouse at least two or three times a week, you're too busy.

GET AWAY!

One woman wrote on a survey, "I wish my husband and I had invested more time and money in our love relationship. The divorce was much more expensive—and much more traumatic for the children than occasional weekends away would have been!"[32]

Sadly, too many couples come to this realization only after they've been through the upheaval of a divorce. I know your kids may whine about missing an occasional game. Your budget may groan while being stretched to make room for that bed-and-breakfast weekend. It's a hassle to find someone to watch the kids. But as a married couple, you simply must get away.

At least once a year I think it's good to get away mainly for sex. Have a weekend where both of you plan to spend a lot of time inside. Enjoy the anticipation—maybe even abstain for a while the week or so before you leave. Plan a sexual feast, without apology and without shame. This is the time to go back through that variety chapter and really think about ways to spice up your love life. Maybe the wife will "shave" for the first time. Maybe the husband will hide a bag of flower petals and strew them across the bed while his lover is taking a shower. Maybe the wife will book a room with mirrors. Maybe the husband will bring along some foot lotion.

In the end, as much as they may complain initially, your kids will thank you for your commitment to loving each other (though of course they'll never know why you really went away).

[32]Sanna with Miller, *How to Romance*, 119.

TAKE CARE OF THE CONFLICTS

Getting a hotel might be beyond some budgets. In fact, some families might groan under the strain of hiring a baby-sitter.

If this is true of you, find a couple who will regularly trade "spot" baby-sitting with you. If you know things have been too rushed, call Julia and say, "Julia, Carter and I really need a couple hours alone, without the kids. Can you watch them from five to seven this evening?"

"Planning a little early evening delight, are we?" Julia may ask.

"I'll be happy to return the favor for you tomorrow or sometime next week," you can reply.

Men, if you feel your wife is too busy to really enjoy sex, surprise her with a coupon for three hours' worth of a housecleaning service, make arrangements for someone to watch the kids, and then let your wife enjoy sexual intimacy before 11 P.M. for one time in her life! Imagine how good it will feel for her to not have to muster the energy after vacuuming the carpets, fixing dinner, washing dishes, bathing two toddlers, getting them to bed, and then trying not to fall asleep out of weariness. Take care of the particulars so your wife can really relax.

MAKE SACRIFICES

One of the most difficult things about being a woman in America today is that everybody wants a piece of you. Your boss wants that memo; the church is looking for "just one" evening a week; the kids want to get to three different locations; teachers want a homeroom helper. Of course, to save up for the kids' college you're also running a Mary Kay business on the side.

If this is even remotely close to describing your life, I can already tell you what your husband would say to me if he were sitting in my counseling room. He might use different words and different images, but in essence he'd say, "If I'm lucky, I get squeezed in between the late news and David Letterman."

I'm not naïve—believe me, I passed naïve a couple decades ago. Thirty years in the counseling business will remove pretty much all pretense. So I realize that what I'm about to say will be difficult for some of you to hear, and very costly for others of you to enact: A good marriage and family life is worth sacrificing for. To preserve time for marital intimacy—not to mention just being available for your kids—you may have to do without a few things. You may have to drive a car for ten years or more. You may have to forgo expensive vacations. You may have to make do with hand-me-downs or shopping in thrift stores rather than going to Nordstrom for the kids' back-to-school shopping.

But the sacrifices will be worth it. I don't say this lightly because I know for some of you, giving up the "finer things in life" will really, really hurt. Without denying the difficulty behind this sacrifice, I still think you'll be most fulfilled by investing more time in your family, even if that means having a much lighter bank account.

A MAN'S ENEMY

For most men, exhaustion is not the greatest enemy of sex. Speaking for my gender, I think it's safe to say that we could be nodding off, having stayed up thirty-six hours without a wink of sleep—but if our wife touches us in just the right place, *boing!* We're ready to go.

For most men, the greatest enemy of sex is a lack of imagination on the part of their wives. If a man doesn't feel pursued or wanted or if his wife is unable or unwilling to communicate how much she enjoys being with him and how much she wants his body, hubby loses interest. Your husband wants to be needed and wanted and prized; he's like a little boy in that regard.

The challenge is, for you to pursue your husband in this way requires time, energy, and foresight—something an overly busy woman simply won't have. But here's the irony. The kind of man who is loved in a fulfilling way is the kind of man who, when his wife calls and asks him to pick up a gallon of milk at the grocery store on his way home—even though he passed that store three miles ago—will go back to that store and get that milk, giving you more time in the process.

When your husband says, "Not a problem," it's because he wants to please his woman. If he feels loved and prized, he'll knock down walls for you.

We've already touched on this, so I won't bore you by getting repetitive. Just remember—if you want a great sex life, you've got to protect your schedule. Make time for unhurried, creative lovemaking.

13

Your Sexual IQ

You know the problem I have with books like this? Too often they act like people lack basic sexual knowledge. Although I've found that to be true for a few couples I've counseled, the fact is, this generation may be the most sexually informed of any generation ever in the history of the world.

By the same measure, however, many couples are woefully ignorant about their *spouse's* particular preferences. Why is this?

One, I think that past sexual experience is counterproductive. A man thinks he knows what "women in general" like, but that stops him from finding out what one particular woman (his wife) really likes. He thinks he's Don Juan, but he doesn't know squat about the sexual interests, fears, hopes, and fantasies of the woman to whom he's married.

In the same way, a woman may know what

pleased her college lover—but that doesn't mean the same thing will please her husband. If she's had multiple lovers, she may even get confused over past memories.

Second, most of our "information" comes to us from the media. The truth is, articles are designed to sell magazines; the reporter didn't actually talk to *your* husband or wife. Those sensational headlines—"Light His Fire with the Secret Spot You Never Knew Existed" or "Make Her Moan All Night Long with a New Position"—are just that: sensational. They may or may not bear any resemblance to the truth.

You won't discover your husband's or wife's favorite places to be touched by reading *Cosmopolitan* or *Esquire*. You have to talk to each other, specifically about sex—something that surprisingly few couples do. We may read about sex more than previous generations did, but not that many couples actually talk about sex.

I'm more concerned about your Sexual IQ as it relates to your partner's personal likes and dislikes than I am about how it might relate to whether you can describe every position. You might be a sexual gymnast, but if your spouse likes it slow, mild, and smooth, all those moves will simply annoy her.

If you don't know the answer to the following questions, spend the next several weeks trying to find out the answers by talking to your spouse. I realize that many of the answers may be "that depends," but don't use this as an excuse. Discuss the circumstances in which the answers will relate. You should know your spouse so well that you could answer many of these questions in many different ways.

1. Does your spouse prefer candlelight, total darkness, mood lights, colored lights, or complete white light during sex? Does she or he like to experiment with light? If so, when, and in what mood?
2. Does your spouse like any particular smells during sex?

Does she enjoy candles? If so, what fragrance? Does he appreciate any special perfume?

3. What is your spouse's favorite time of the day to engage in sexual relations? Do you ever make room in your schedule to accommodate this time?

4. Does your spouse like you to talk during sex? Make more noise during sex? Does he or she want you to talk more before you have sex? Would she or he prefer that you start praying before or after sex on occasion?

5. Does your wife have a favorite massage lotion? Does she like the lotion heated, or straight out of the bottle?

6. Does your spouse like to have fun during sex, or is he or she more serious?

7. What are your spouse's three favorite places to be touched? kissed?

8. What position is your spouse's favorite?

9. What is one sexual practice your spouse would really like to try that the two of you haven't done yet?

10. What is your spouse's favorite sexual fantasy?

11. What turns off your spouse quicker than anything else?

SEXUAL COMMUNICATION

In my practice I've found that most couples spend 99.9 percent of their sexual relationship making love, and .1 percent talking about it. I wish it would be more like 90 percent–10 percent. Oh, couples may joke about sex, but what I'm referring to as "talk" is a substantive discussion where the two of you really share your heart about what you like and don't like in your sex life. Even married couples—who have seen everything there is to see—may still find it extremely embarrassing and difficult to actually talk about sexual likes and dislikes.

Part of this comes, of course, from a hesitancy about making our spouse feel bad. Who wants to hear that they're not good in bed? And who wants to be the one who says it?

So what usually happens is that relatively simple remedies go ignored. Some spouses put up with something they don't like for a decade or more because they're afraid to bring it up; they don't want to hurt their spouse. Others have denied themselves something for years because they're too embarrassed to ask for it.

One of the best things you can do to improve your sex life is learn how to talk . . . I mean *really talk.*

Bringing Up Difficult Topics

Dr. Judith Reichman lists several conversation starters that will help you address potentially embarrassing or hurtful topics:[33]

- "I know it can be embarrassing talking about sex, but we're both adults."
- "I have something to say, but I find it difficult to talk about."
- "You may have noticed that I've been avoiding situations where we would have sex."
- "You don't seem to be in the mood for sex lately. Is there anything you want to talk about?"
- "Have you noticed that we've fallen into a routine when it comes to sex? Do you ever think about us being more adventurous?"
- "It's harder for me to get aroused these days. I'm not sure why, but I was hoping we could talk about it."

Here's another approach to consider:

"This is uncomfortable, and I'm not even sure it's accurate, but this is how I feel . . ." I like this softening approach because it tends to diffuse accusations and anger. A similar angle is this: "I could be wrong, but . . ."

[33]Reichman, *I'm Not in the Mood*, 142–143.

Here's a sample conversation starter that a woman might use if her husband doesn't practice good hygiene:

"Honey, so many times, you want to make love to me, but you haven't showered. You don't come to bed smelling clean and fresh, and you know me, I've got a nose like a beagle. I love the smell of your hair when it's just been shampooed. But too often, you smell like work. I love you to pieces and I love to be with you.

"It's hard for me to tell you this because I don't want to hurt your feelings, but if you would just shower, that would make me much more willing to please you."

The brilliance of this woman's approach is that she put the onus on herself ("You know me, I've got a nose like a beagle") and she also put a positive spin on it ("that would make me much more willing to please you").

Most men should welcome such conversations.

The Daring Question

Telling your spouse you're not happy with your sexual life is about one of the most painful things you can do. Sometimes it's necessary, *but it still hurts.* You can mention any number of positives—"I love the way you kiss; I love the way you use your hands; I love the way you're creative." But the one negative—"Sometimes you seem a little passive"—is the *only* thing your spouse will remember you saying.

There's a way around this. The Schwambachs call this phrase "Ten Magic Words."[34] I like to call it the daring question. But the brilliance of it is that it puts a request in a positive frame. It allows you to break new ground without hurting your spouse or suggesting he or she hasn't been good enough.

Ready? Here it goes: "Do you know what I would love to try sometime?"

[34]The Schwambachs talk about this in their book *For Lovers Only* (Eugene, Ore.: Harvest House, 1990), 239ff.

If you say these words with the right tone, you can turn it into foreplay. The mere thought becomes erotic and inviting.

If you hear your spouse say these words to you, your reaction is so important. First, understand that it may have taken him or her days or even weeks to build up the courage to say this. A casual dismissal: "What are you, some kind of pervert?" "You can't be serious; you're joking, right? *Right?*" will pretty much shut down all future communication.

Instead, it's your responsibility at least to consider the request (provided it's not immoral or degrading). You may not be comfortable with it, but at least try to sound excited and consider how much courage it took your spouse to bring it up. Then try to rephrase it in a light that sounds inviting to you:

"You know what, honey, that sounds wonderful to me, too. Why don't you take a bath before you come to bed tonight and we'll see what happens?"

The example the Schwambachs use is a good one. Let's say your husband rushes from the top to the bottom, and you really enjoy having your breasts fondled, caressed, and kissed. Instead of saying, "Why are you always in such a rush? Haven't you ever heard of foreplay?" try, "You know what I'd love to try sometime?"

"What, honey?"

"I wonder how excited you could make me just by making love to my breasts. Use everything you've got—your mouth, your hands, even Mr. Happy. Get creative, and let's see how far we go."

What's important is that the woman is saying, *I want to be turned on, and I want to be turned on by you.* That's what will drive a man wild. When your husband sees how excited you become as he caresses and fondles you, you won't be able to get him off your breasts with a crowbar. He'll take it as a challenge and will certainly want to finish the job.

THE PSYCHOLOGY OF SEDUCTION

Related to your sexual IQ is how well you know what gets your partner in the mood. Those who study these things have determined that there are four areas of seduction: visual (where a person becomes sexually excited by what he or she sees); kinesthetic (where a person becomes aroused through touch); auditory (where a person is titillated by sound); and relational (where a person is attracted by emotional care and nurture).

Now, all of us are liable to be aroused by any and all of these four at various times—but most people favor one over the others.

Let me ask you this: Which one most excites your spouse?

You don't know? You've been married how long?

The sad truth is, these basic things often go ignored in many marriages. Find out what sexual language your spouse most wants you to speak. Throw in some variety, but always favor his or her primary attraction.

Key to understanding this is the psychology behind seduction. It's all about presentation. I want to ask you something: describe for me the last twenty or thirty sexual interludes you've had with your mate. What were they like? I'll bet some wives could describe them to a T. You know why? Because most of those episodes were just like all the rest: number three was just like number nine was just like number twenty-seven.

Couples settle in. They become creatures of habit. They forget about the little details.

I watch a good bit of sports—and I attend many of the contests. You see a lot in warm-up that you don't see on television. Wise, seasoned, and successful coaches know that appearance and presentation matter. Yes, you need the substance to back it up, but a team can be intimidated before any individual player touches a ball. That's a big psychological advantage.

When it comes to sex, how you present yourself is crucial. It's almost a cliché to talk about a couple's disagreements over a woman's sleepwear. Most wives wear something to bed that is far more "functional" than men wish it was. My wife has pajamas with feet and no trap door! That's okay–I guess–for those cold winter nights when you know nothing is going to happen. But let me give you a glimpse into the male psyche.

There's this thing we men talk about called "headlights." When you're a young boy watching the women's Olympic diving competition, for example, you might get together with your buddies and mention one swimmer's "amazing headlights."

What are we talking about?

Nipples. When a man can see a woman's nipples through the fabric she is wearing, it turns us into goo. We melt all over the floor. I can't explain it, but I can describe it. We get weak in the knees at the right presentation.

Don't get me wrong: I don't want to see the imprints of another woman's nipples. I want to see the ones I have access to. One presentation is teasing and provocative, but it can't be fulfilled so it's really frustrating and cruel. But the other presentation, well, that's the doorway to delight! I don't know anything more alluring than a satiny top being pushed from underneath by your wife's two nipples. A lot of men would jog five miles just to see that in their own bedroom.

Now here's how you build on the presentation. Let's say your husband hears the shower running at 10:30 P.M. Just the sound of the water makes him a bit frisky. When he hears that shower turn on, he's thinking, *Oh man, I could get lucky tonight.* When his wife walks out sporting a new nightie that conveniently displays those headlights, he's suddenly a little boy.

"Wow! Is that new?"

Now here's the smart woman. She looks him right in the

eye, bends toward him to let her breasts work their magic, and then says, "I got it just for you."

That scenario alone could bring a good number of American men straight to orgasm!

Yes, it's expensive. Maybe the entire getup cost you fifty bucks. It was well worth it. Many families pay five hundred dollars for a television, and that doesn't do a thing for their marriage.

My wife, Sande, is a master of the artful presentation. When Sande gives women a gift, most hate to open it because the gift wrapping looks so immaculate. They think it would be a shame to mess it up! I've sat and marveled at how women will go on and on about how attractive a gift looks that Sande has wrapped. You should see our dinner table at Christmas—not only is the food good, but it looks *great*.

In fact, people drive to Tucson from one hundred miles away or more to visit my wife's store, Shabby Hattie. Why? Sande knows how to present old stuff in a way that knocks women out. She can turn an old lampshade into a work of art by recovering it with just the right fabric. Target also sells lampshades, but not too many people would drive one hundred miles to visit one. Why? It all comes down to presentation.

Ladies, learn how to present yourself—to wrap yourself, to wrap your room, to wrap the moment in a seductive allure tailor-made to your husband.

Now, men, you could use a little help here, too. We've already talked about good hygiene. When you wear dress socks to bed, or snuggle under the covers in underwear you've been wearing all day long, you're not exactly overwhelming in your sex appeal.

Keep in mind that "presentation" to your wife is broader than just your body. You could make love in the garage and not even notice the gasoline can and dirty hammer lying at your feet—but your wife probably isn't that way. Just as a wife can present herself in an alluring way coming out of a shower by wearing something that shows her headlights, so you can present yourself in an alluring way by greeting your wife with pleasant surroundings.

Here's a practical example. Let's say your wife left the house in a mess to go to an all-day seminar. She's been gone for seven hours, and, quite frankly, is dreading what the house will look like when she gets back. She knows she left it a mess, but even worse, she knows you and the kids have been living in it all day long. She expects she'll have to cook up some fish sticks for a late dinner, and she can imagine staying up past midnight trying to clean everything up.

Now imagine her surprise when she walks into a clean house, with kids who are bathed and put to bed on time. She can't believe her sense of smell—you've got her favorite salad with her favorite salad dressing sitting on the table, and a perfectly cooked fillet of halibut topped with just the right spices.

Once she's finished with dinner, you take her plate and invite her to go upstairs. She walks into the bathroom, only to find that you've laid out some candles and bath salts and a nice, new, fluffy bath towel. She eases into the hot water and feels delicious.

That, my dear male readers, is the equivalent of a wife walking out showing her headlights. Yeah, in some ways we're easier to please than they are—but oh, that extra work is certainly worth the effort.

14

Too Pooped to Whoop

*I*magine this: The chief of staff knocks on the president's door. "Mr. President, it's time for you to deliver the State of the Union Address."

"Thanks, Andy," the president says. "But you know what? I don't really feel like giving a speech tonight. Think I'll pass."

Or this: The coach of the St. Louis Rams calls up quarterback Kurt Warner on a Sunday afternoon in January. "Kurt," the coach says, "the Super Bowl starts in thirty minutes. Where are you?"

"I just don't feel like playing today, Coach. You'll have to make do without me."

Here's a third scenario: Katie Couric's producer from the *Today* show gives her a frantic call at 7:30 in the morning. "Katie, we're supposed to be on the air! What gives?"

Can you imagine Katie saying, "I thought sleep was more important than work today"?

As far-out as these scenarios might sound, they have one thing in common: People have made a commitment, and they are expected to keep that commitment regardless of how they feel. I'm sure that some mornings, Katie really *would* like to sleep in. And I'm equally certain that sometimes the president would like to postpone a major speech. But both of them have made promises, and they're expected to keep those promises.

I wish people had the same attitude when it comes to marriage. When you agreed to marry this man or this woman, you put yourself in a position to meet a need in his or her life that no other person can legitimately meet—sexual fulfillment. I'm blunt with premarital couples: If you're not willing to commit yourself to having sex with this person two to three times a week for the rest of your life, don't get married. Certainly, pregnancy and sickness and a few other unforeseen problems will alter this—but in general, to get married is to commit to a regular time of sexual intimacy.

This means that not being "in the mood" is an interesting sidelight, but it should never determine your actions. You made a commitment, and you'll need to be faithful to that commitment. It's too late to undo it now.

It goes both ways, of course. I tell men that to get married is to commit to regular times of communication. I've *never* met a man who told me, "What I really need after spending a long day at work is a good forty-five-minute talk with my wife." But I tell men that if their wife needs that forty-five-minute conversation, they need to work at providing it.

"But how, Dr. Leman? How can I participate sexually without any real desire?" I'm glad you asked. It shows you're willing to take the first few steps. Here are a few ideas to help you overcome lagging desire.

REMEMBER YOUR COMMITMENT

First, don't panic. Just about every spouse—men and women—will hit this crossroad one time or another. All of us have times when we're tired, preoccupied, or not feeling very close to our spouse. But a good marriage calls us to rise above our apathy. Good old Peter says, "Love each other deeply" (1 Peter 4:8, NIV). Another interpretation for that is "Love each other *at full strength.*" I like that thought—it means I'm not going to give my spouse my half-best; I'm going to use my full strength to please her, giving her everything I've got.

This means there may be times when you have sex out of mercy, obligation, or commitment and without any real desire. Yes, it may feel forced. It might feel planned, and you may fight to stop yourself from just shoving your partner away and saying, "Enough already!"

But the root issue is this: You're acting out of love. You're honoring your commitment. And that's a wonderful thing to do.

REMEMBER THAT SEXUAL INTEREST BUILDS

One of the nice things about sex is that if you'll just "lean into it" for a few minutes, your hesitation can quickly evolve into desperation—and I'm talking about the fun kind of desperation!

Think about it. Haven't you ever had times when sex was the last thing on your mind, but you gave in. Thirty minutes later you're on the verge of an orgasm crying out, "Don't stop! Don't stop! *Please* don't stop!"?

Your husband might remind you that half an hour earlier the last thing you wanted to do was *start. Now* the last thing you want to do is stop. Sex can be like that, if we let it.

Now, some of you may be saying, "No, I've *never* cried out, 'Please don't stop!' because sex is *never* that fulfilling for me."

Sex may not be that way now, but it can *become* like that if you're willing to work at it. Remember: Your Creator specifically designed you to enjoy fulfilling, pleasurable sex, complete with orgasms. Life experience, psychological hang-ups, and sexual inexperience or ignorance can get in the way of your experiencing such pleasure, but the potential for that pleasure remains.

"Convince Me"

If your husband is clearly in the mood and brings up the notion of sex, but you're not even close to desiring it, let him do some of the preparation work. Be straightforward but encouraging by saying, "You know, I'm not really in the mood—but I'll let you try to get me there." That provides him with the opportunity to start romancing you, being affectionate, and warming you up.

Guys, when your wife says this, she's not talking about you immediately diving into her blouse or pants—she wants you to romance her and dine her. Whisper sweet things to her. Instead of saying, "I'm so hot for you," tell her *why* you're hot and *what* you're hot about. Make it *personal* with sincere compliments.

And then take the time to let her warm up. Get out some lotion and offer a nice relaxing massage. A foot rub or a back rub or even a total body massage might really hit the jackpot! Tell her that you'll tuck the kids into bed while she takes a bath. Provide an atmosphere where romance has a chance to blossom.

Find Rituals That Put You in the Mood

You're a complete person. Stress, weariness, and other factors can cause sexual disinterest. Fight back with proven rituals that put you in the mood. Many women enjoy a long process of bathing, applying lotion, and putting on some soft robe.

You might find that certain books or music put you in the mood. (I'm not talking about pornography!) Sometimes reading books like this one, which discuss sex in an appropriate way, can get your mind (and other parts of you) humming.

I know one young man who said he'd promise to control

his thought life, and then asked in return that his wife control her thought life by thinking about sex *more*.

"What do you mean?" she asked.

"Just try to think about it more often," he said.

Fantasies about your spouse are entirely appropriate. Remind yourself of special nights. Dream up something that hasn't been done before. Direct your thoughts toward your spouse.

Foreplay Begins in the Morning

Some of the best sex lasts all day, even though both partners may spend the first ten hours of that day ten miles apart.

Imagine what a man would feel like if he woke up, stumbled into the bathroom, turned on the light, and picked up his razor, only to be startled by some vivid writing in red lipstick at the corner of the mirror:

"Good morning, Mr. Sexy! Let's put the kids to bed early tonight. I've got some exciting plans! XOXOXO."

A husband could tape a short note to the mirror:

"Good morning, beautiful. Have I told you lately how much I love your gorgeous eyes?"

My point is to begin foreplay early in the morning to help both of you get in the mood. Make sex an all-day affair.

Exercise

Studies have shown that moderate exercise raises endorphins and may increase intensity of sexual arousal.[35] Just feeling more fit makes you feel better overall, but a workout really can help put you in the mood.

There's a limit to this, however. Excessive workouts—such as training for a marathon, for example, or prolonged bike-riding (which can contribute to clitoral numbness)—can tire you out and reduce sexual interest.

[35]Reichman, *I'm Not in the Mood*, 138.

ONE ISN'T NECESSARILY A LONELY NUMBER

Pleasing each other sexually doesn't need to include intercourse. There are times for whatever reason that a wife may choose to make use of what younger men affectionately refer to as "hand jobs."

A woman with heavy periods that last six or seven days, or who has just gotten through a pregnancy, or perhaps is simply not feeling her best, may genuinely feel that sex is more than she can handle. But with a minimum of effort, she can help her husband who feels like he's about ready to climb the walls because it's been so long.

It works both ways: If a husband lacks the interest but the wife is aroused, he can wrap his arms around her, spooning her on the outside, and let his index finger express his affection.

My point is that if you truly love each other, you'll find a way to take care of each other. There are going to be times when one partner is getting pleased and the other is doing the pleasing. Once again, that's an unselfish and very caring thing to do.

FEMALE SEXUAL PROBLEMS

The American Psychiatric Association divides female sexual problems into four categories:[36]

Sexual Desire Disorder occurs when a person loses all interest in sexual intimacy, or even develops an aversion to it. Everyone has moments when they're not interested, but those suffering from this disorder are chronically uninterested and persistently avoid or respond disfavorably to sexual stimulation. These individuals never heat up. Not only do they lack desire, the mere thought of sex becomes distasteful.

Sexual Arousal Disorder occurs when a woman may *desire* sex, but physically, her body fails to maintain a state of

[36]Reichman, *I'm Not in the Mood*, 38–39.

arousal. She becomes dry and/or unresponsive to sexual stimulation. Her mind is engaged, but her body can never quite seem to catch up.

Orgasmic Disorder results when a woman cannot reach sexual climax after a normal progression of sexual activity. She may enjoy herself, and the desire for orgasm is there, but she never quite "falls off the cliff" and is perpetually left hanging. Since it is rare for a woman to reach orgasm every time she engages in sexual relations, diagnosing any particular individual with this disorder is somewhat arbitrary. Realistically, most women cannot expect to always experience orgasm. Health and age issues will also affect this outcome.

Sexual Pain Disorder means a woman experiences chronic vaginal pain during intercourse. This pain is not due to an infection or a known medical condition. In some cases, there is an involuntary tightening of the muscles on the outside of the vagina that causes the discomfort.

Never one to make things easy, the APA adds a variety of classifications for each disorder. Some may be psychological, while others may be medical. Some could be lifelong (it's always been that way, ever since the woman became sexually active); others are "acquired." They can also be generalized (happening universally) or situational (with a particular partner or under certain circumstances).

Dr. Judith Reichman has identified a number of "sexual saboteurs" for women that lead to and build on these disorders.[37] Among her findings are:

1. Psychological issues
Guilt, depression, stress, anxiety—all of these act like weights on a wife's sexual interest and performance. Sometimes these factors are temporary; a woman going through a stressful time at work or stressed out with toddlers may experience a tempo-

[37]Reichman, *I'm Not in the Mood*, 47ff.

rary reduction in her sexual desire. Other times, long-standing psychological pressure can make the lack of desire chronic.

Prior sexual abuse is another psychological time bomb. Almost one-fourth of all females will be sexually abused by the time they reach adulthood, and the residual effects of this tragic behavior are wide-sweeping and, in some cases, lifelong. Any sexual activity can cause flashbacks or memories. In some cases, the trauma is buried much deeper, and while there may not be any actual memories, a buried aversion to sexual activity just won't go away.

As much as I'd like to help you, it would be irresponsible for me as a therapist to give you five quick steps to overcome such a history. If you are one of the 25 percent who have been sexually abused in your past, I strongly recommend that you seek out professional counseling. This is something that needs expert care. The good news is that I personally have witnessed many women move past ambivalent or even hostile feelings toward sex—arising because of previous abuse—and after months of counseling, hard work, and sympathetic care by their husbands, now enjoy fulfilling sexual intimacy.

Another psychological issue—though one not mentioned by Reichman—is premarital sexual activity. Since many experts consider this activity to be normal, it is rarely addressed as a factor in a woman's struggle to become more sexually responsive. This is tragic, as I have found guilt over previous sexual experiences, and a sense of being bound to previous sexual partners, to be one of the most common hindrances to a greater enjoyment of sex within marriage.

In fact, I talked to one couple where the wife confessed that premarital sexual activity kept her inhibited in bed for the first seven years of their marriage. What might surprise some readers is that both she and her husband were virgins on their wedding night, but they had "pushed the envelope" of what the wife was comfortable with before they got married. This resulted in her having a difficult time trusting her husband in bed, and it was only after she brought it up and he asked her for her forgiveness that she was finally able to fully enjoy sexual intimacy.

Premarital sex comes with a high price tag—spiritually and psychologically, it can be a major drain on sex after marriage. If this is part of your history, you will want to see a good counselor or perhaps discuss this with a wise pastor.

2. Couple Issues

When a relationship goes bad, or simply cools off, it's only a matter of time until the sexual fervor follows suit. When a husband gets too involved in his work, or when a wife starts ignoring her marriage because she is enamored with her children, eventually sexual interest will wane. The relationship is dying, and sex is often a barometer of that death.

When a man dominates and controls, or a woman manipulates or gossips, the partner may simply lose any feelings of affection. I often shock women's groups by telling them that 80 percent or more of them have broken their marriage vows to "cherish their spouse" in the previous week. They often act like that's just ridiculous—until I inform them that talking about the specifics of their sexual relationship with their spouse, or even the details of a fight, with a girlfriend or family member is seen by most men as a violation of their privacy. And that certainly doesn't make a man (or woman) feel cherished or safe in a relationship.

When a man is condescending, talking down to his wife and perhaps even blatantly calling her stupid, it's no wonder sexual interest wanes. When a woman tries to control her husband or even tries to use sex to get her way, it's not surprising that hubby quickly grows tired of playing that game.

The best sex takes place in the best and healthiest relationships. It's not something that exists in a vacuum. It's a serious mistake to focus on sexual technique when the relationship is the root problem. For more on this, please read my book *Sex Begins in the Kitchen*.

3. Drugs

Surprisingly, not enough research has been done in this area. We still have more work to do when it comes to exploring and understanding the link between medications and sexual desire. Since more people are on medication today than perhaps at any other time in history, the link is certainly something worth exploring if you experience your own drop in desire.

Reichman writes,

> Many drugs have both a direct effect on our brain and central nervous system and a local effect on our genitalia, and on occasion that drug's action on one may contradict its effect on the other. For example, an antidepressant might boost our mood and make us more likely to want sex, yet if it increases serotonin levels in the brain we wind up with lowered libido. Birth control pills might correct certain hormonal imbalances but may also diminish testosterone levels and libido. On a more local basis, some women find birth control pills increase vaginal lubrication while others find the opposite to be true, especially if they develop more yeast infections and pain with intercourse.[38]

Obviously, this is an area where you need to consult your physician. Consider birth control, hormone replacement therapy, antidepressants, tranquilizers, and blood-pressure medicine as possible culprits. Even antacids, antibiotics, and antihistamines can fool around with your libido.

[38]Reichman, *I'm Not in the Mood*, 61–62.

4. Disease

Multiple sclerosis, diabetes, cancer, arthritis, thyroid problems, and the like all present individual challenges to sexual intimacy. In the case of multiple sclerosis, for example, arousal can be blocked and vaginal dryness can make intercourse less pleasurable. In the case of epilepsy, it's often the therapy, and not the disease, that causes lack of sexual interest. If you are being treated for a medical condition, talk to your doctor about ways to address your lack of sexual interest.

5. Pain

Men, would you enjoy sexual intercourse if it felt like someone was jabbing you in the penis with a needle every time you entered your wife? Of course not. Some women feel ashamed when sex is painful, and they may even try to mask their discomfort, but few things block sexual desire like pain.

Pain can erupt from any number of causes: vaginal dryness, vaginal constriction, arthritis, or even sore muscles. For dryness, use one of many available lubricants, such as K-Y jelly, Astroglide, Lubrin, or something similar. Some women need this more than others; most will need it at some points in their lives and on certain occasions or times of the month.

A woman's naturally declining level of estrogen as she ages can also create more vaginal dryness. Some doctors prescribe hormones to address this problem, but not everyone is comfortable taking hormones. In these cases, the topical lubricants can help.

Whatever the cause, a woman should see her doctor immediately if sex has become (or certainly if it has always been) painful. You shouldn't have to suffer. Both the husband and wife are served most when the wife enjoys times of sexual intimacy. I don't know many men who get turned on by the thought of a woman "grinning and bearing it."

WHEN HUBBY ISN'T INTERESTED

The stereotype is that the man is the one who usually wants sex, but I've talked to many couples where the man has less sexual interest than his wife. I've worked with more of these couples than you might expect. One time a woman came to see me who was knockout gorgeous. If she walked by a building project, I guarantee you that absolutely no work would get done until she was out of sight. Even so, her husband wouldn't touch her.

Sometimes the problem lies with gender identification issues. Other times men are simply desperate for control—so desperate, in fact, that they insist the wife always initiates. That way, the men are never turned down. In most instances, however, the husband is simply tired, or preoccupied, or maybe a little depressed.

Here are a few things the wife can do to help heat hubby up.

Dress Slowly

Men are turned on by sight, so you can get your husband thinking about sex first thing in the morning by taking your time getting dressed—in full view. Walk out of the shower when he's in the bedroom, and drop the towel on your way to the closet. Maybe give him a hug, but don't make him think you expect anything.

Don't be in a hurry to cover up. Choose either the top or the bottom, but get dressed in such a way that one or the other stays in full view for as long as possible. Put on your panties and then your skirt, keeping your top bare, for instance. Comb out your hair before you put your bra on. Let him see what he's missing.

If you really want to get him going, ask him to help you clasp your bra in back. Of course you know how to do it; you do it every day! But men can be slow in such matters. Say something like, "My fingers feel uncoordinated today—can you hook my bra for me?" He'll be none the wiser, but maybe a little more interested.

Plant Polaroids

Because men are visual, sight becomes a powerful ally in your mission to sexually charge your husband.

In the morning, plant a self-taken portrait of yourself in a bathrobe, and tape it to the mirror where he shaves. Write on it in lipstick, "Good morning, honey!"

Then, throughout the day, plant additional Polaroids, each one going a step further in your stage of undress. These can be planted in a briefcase, a lunchbox, and then in his closet where he changes when he gets home. The idea is that by bedtime, he'll have seen a virtual strip show—but you've saved the best parts until last.

This one is a bit costly, of course—it requires a Polaroid camera with a self-timer on it, but I'm sure you and your husband can find other creative uses for that device. (You can also use a digital camera, which will allow you to print pictures without anyone else seeing them.)

Dealing with Impotence

Men and women both need to become aware of the vagaries of impotence. It's bound to happen in any marriage eventually. The statistics are pretty telling: While just 5 to 7 percent of the male population experiences impotence in their twenties, one-fourth of all men sixty-five and older have struggles in this area. After the age of seventy, one out of every two men share this struggle.[39]

The failure to achieve a satisfying erection can be partial (somewhat erect, but not entirely; or erect, followed by a quick softening) and occasional, or total and chronic. It can be psychological or physiological.

[39]Reichman, *I'm Not in the Mood*, 94.

Any disease or medication that reduces blood flow to the penis can create occasional or chronic impotence; hypertension, coronary vascular disease, and diabetes are all culprits (half of all men diagnosed with diabetes will experience some form of erectile dysfunction within five years of their first diagnosis).[40] A decreasing level of testosterone and the normal process of aging may also be contributing factors.

From a psychologist's perspective, I think it's important to keep a level head about this. An occasional lapse is nothing to be concerned about. In fact, getting overly concerned about it is a good way to create a psychological form of impotence.

Secondly, don't take out your anger on your spouse over what your body isn't doing. Don't assume your inability to respond physically is an indictment of your sex life. It might simply be reality finally settling in. By all means, get a physical checkup, see a counselor, consider ways to keep sex fun and fresh; but don't assume there's necessarily anything wrong with you or your partner just because Mr. Happy occasionally refuses to do anything but frown.

I'm not a medical doctor, but sometimes doctors will refer patients to me if they have ruled out physical causes for impotence and believe the reasons are more psychological. If you occasionally wake up with an erection but can't become erect during the act of lovemaking, the cause is less likely to be physical. If you become hard but then grow soft as soon as you think about penetration, once again, it's likely that the cause is something happening within the relationship rather than your body. You may be anxious about your performance, working through some anger, or something else.

If, however, you've gradually lost the ability to get and maintain an erection over the years, until now you hardly become erect at all, you very well may be facing a medical condi-

[40]Reichman, *I'm Not in the Mood,* 95.

tion that needs a diagnosis. A good doctor can help you rule out any physical causes. Once you have a clean bill of health, you can work on improving the relationship. In this day and age, with Viagra and many other options available to couples, impotence needn't sideline most marriages.

DEAL WITH IT!

Whatever the cause behind your own lack of sexual desire, please, for the sake of your marriage, deal with it! It's just not healthy for a marriage for either partner to show a consistent and persistent lack of sexual desire. It's only a matter of time until the spouse takes this lack of desire personally. To be fair, it's only natural to do so.

To add insult to injury, you're also denying your spouse the joy and fulfillment of having someone who is pursuing him or her sexually. From a faith perspective, it's not morally permissible for anyone else to fulfill this role. If you don't do it, nobody else can. Your denial means your spouse will have to go without.

By all means, get aggressive in your desire to become well. Go to a good counselor. Deal with the issues that are holding you back. Don't accept the status quo if your disinterest is causing disharmony and frustration in your marriage.

You might keep telling yourself, "I'll deal with it—someday." But eventually, your spouse may say, "Enough is enough!" I've seen too many marriages destroyed by lack of sexual desire on the part of one spouse or the other.

Remember: Feelings are important and valid, but you're not a slave to them. Just because you don't feel like having sex doesn't mean you can't choose to have sex—at least, in some form. Maybe you really are too tired to have intercourse—but are you willing to please your husband in other ways?

You made a promise; are you going to keep it?

Sex in the Winter

I have a couple of friends who have demonstrated their loyalty to me for many years. They've never given me any trouble. They are the trustworthiest, most comfortable, agreeable, and durable friends ever put on two feet.

I love my slippers.

Sande hates them.

On at least five different occasions, I've caught my wife trying to kidnap my friends and send them off to the garbage dump—but I'm too quick for her. I've been able to rescue those guys every single time.

Following the most recent rescue, Sande made an emotional appeal: "Kevin, why do you insist on wearing those ugly, beat-up slippers?"

"They're comfortable."

"Those things are just gross; they're covered in dirt and paint and beyond repair. You should just get rid of them."

"Get rid of them?" I asked her. "Just because they're old? Just because they have a little wear and tear? What kind of attitude is that?" I asked her. After all, how would she like to be traded in for another woman, just because she isn't in her twenties anymore? I'd never do that, just as I'd never part with my favorite pair of slippers. Old doesn't mean inferior, just as new doesn't mean better.

When I talk about "sex in the winter," I'm *not* referring to heating up the sheets between December and February. I'm talking about enjoying satisfying sexual intimacy in your forties, fifties, sixties, and beyond.

I might be biased because I've only been with one woman, but in my humble opinion I think sex actually gets better as a couple ages. I realize this isn't always the case. I spoke rather recently to a sixty-five-year-old man who hadn't slept with his wife in over ten years. I can't imagine going ten *weeks*, much less ten years, without having sex with my wife. But the truth is, what age takes away, it often compensates for by giving other qualities back.

Certainly sex changes. As we move into our fifties and beyond, our bodies may not be quite as tight—but our vision isn't so great either, so both weaknesses kind of cancel each other out! We may not have the same stamina we once did, and our limbs may not be nearly so flexible as they were in our twenties. But on the positive side, we have a lifetime of experience in pleasing this one person. We have the ability to control our responses to a better degree, often leading to longer lovemaking. And we have the immeasurable advantage of intuitively reading our spouse's moans, because we've been with him or her for decades.

Another big plus is that once the kids move out, there is usually more freedom, more leisure time, and often more money. Many couples hit the empty nest in their forties and almost certainly by their fifties. In our case we'll be empty nesters at the "hottie" age of seventy-two! It's easier to get away, and as you've probably already picked up by now, I'm a big proponent of hotel sex for married couples!

TURNING THE CORNER

First, let me say, *expect change*. Face it: Men, you're losing some or even most of your hair. You've probably put on some significant weight. You can't jump as high as you used to. Even Michael Jordan proved that the most athletic among us can't defy the dulling effects of aging.

Women, you've noticed that gravity governs more than heavenly bodies—it has a startling effect on earth as well. Your face, your breasts, and other parts of you seem eager to hit the floor. You may find that you need more lubrication during sex than you ever did before. Your hair, once so full and complete, so blond or so ravishingly black, is now not quite so thick—and what's that white strand? It isn't paint, sister; it's the effects of time.

You've watched as everything about you has changed with time, so why would you think sex wouldn't be affected as well?

It will.

The intensity and pleasure you experience while having sex in your later years doesn't need to diminish, but *how* you approach it will need to be revised. When Michael Jordan came back to the NBA, he was certainly no longer "air Jordan," dropping our jaws with gravity-defying dunks. One coach even began referring to him as "floor Jordan." Sure, he could still play, but his feet were rooted firmly on the ground. He had to find other ways—head feints, jump shots, and the like—to score.

The same thing will be true for you sexually. If you're willing to make a few adaptations for age, you will find—as many couples have—that sex actually can get better in your forties, fifties, and sixties.

WHAT'S GOING TO CHANGE FOR MEN

In your teens and twenties, you could become erect reading a magazine about automobile engines. Just jumping into a pool or passing a pretty girl was sufficient to make your body respond. All your wife had to do to stimulate you to an erection was climb into bed.

In fact, your erections might have come so easily that the two of you may have developed some habits in which your wife rarely gave you much additional stimulation. In fact, when you were quite young, she may have found that too much stimulation could bring things to a rapid end. One wife, Angie, admitted to me that foreplay had been one-sided for years, for the simple reason that just about any foreplay would cause her young husband to climax before they even had sex.

Those were the old days, my friend. Now your erections will need to be cultivated and maintained. If your wife ignores you, you'll go soft. Both of you will need to focus on enjoying and receiving, and that means you are going to need more direct penile stimulation than you used to receive.

Be warned: Mr. Happy may not smile quite as often. He may wilt just when you were hoping he'd stand at full attention. He may resist all efforts at any encore attempted within twenty-four hours, and he certainly won't be the dutiful servant he was in your teens and twenties.

Your erections, once they arrive, will also be different, just as mattresses are. Some mattresses compete with boards for their hardness; others resemble pillows. Well, men, the time is going to come when you won't be bringing a two-by-four to bed. Think "pine" instead of "oak." You'll still be hard, but not as hard as you used to be.

As you age, you may also discover something you never could have imagined in your twenties: sex without ejaculation. Older men simply don't need to climax as often as younger men do. The upside of this is that you'll probably be able to last longer and perhaps please your partner more. The downside is that wives may be horrified that the tables have turned and now there's a question about whether *you* will reach orgasm. Ladies, it's not a failure on your part if your man makes love to you for twenty or thirty minutes, yet never climaxes. It doesn't mean he's not attracted to you or that he doesn't find you sexually appealing—it simply means his body is getting older.

Recovery time will slow down as well. The honeymoon nights, where you were able to have several orgasms in the space of a few hours, won't come nearly as easily. It will take longer for your body to recover from your last sexual experience before you are ready to climax again. This change will be gradual and come in waves, but as you march toward your sixties, it's inevitable. (In fact, for some of you it may come in your late forties.) When this season hits, some of you may need to wait hours; others may need to wait for days. But you will need to wait.

There's a big advantage to all of this. On occasion, women enjoy a "quickie" just as much as men, but as a staple, they tend to prefer longer, slower, more languid times of sexual intimacy. Well, welcome to winter—finally, your body is going to match your wife's. You'll be able to last longer. You'll be freer to concentrate on your wife's response. And you can become a much better lover than that twenty-two-year-old stud you used to be (or thought you were).

If erection problems persist, keep in mind there may well be an underlying physical cause, such as arteriosclerosis or some other medical condition. It could be some medication you're on or extra stress you're under. That's why I recommend you get a full physical checkup if erectile problems begin to surface. In the age of Viagra and many other options, impotence is nowhere near the issue it used to be.

Let me say a word to the women who are married to aging

men: Please keep in mind, ladies, that an occasional failure to perform can become a psychological rut if either partner over-reacts. Don't take these changes personally, and certainly don't make them become even more repetitive by putting increased pressure on your husband to perform.

I also want you women to understand that you're at a distinct advantage in this regard: You've grown up knowing that sexual interest can wax and wane, sort of like the tide at the beach. Your husband is used to going from zero to sixty in a steady, speedy climb, and then driving off a cliff! You'll have to help him understand how to keep loving in the midst of an occasional valley, because he may never have been in a valley before.

Also, it's only natural that he feels his problem is bigger than yours. If you fail to lubricate naturally, you can keep receiving pleasure and hang in there until you "warm up." Failing that, you can always reach for the bottle of Astroglide or a tube of K-Y jelly.

The man, on the other hand, knows there will be no intercourse if he doesn't become hard. And that can be a terrifying thought, because just as you can't force yourself to lubricate, he can't force himself to become erect. Of course, every counselor knows that worrying over this will tend to reinforce the problem rather than solve it, but when a man isn't used to dealing with these issues, even confronting them one time can become a real source of concern.

If it doesn't appear that your husband is going to be ready for intercourse and wants to continue pleasing you either manually or orally, *please let him.* For starters, the sight of you reaching orgasm may be enough to make him become erect. But even if it doesn't, a man wants to know he can please his wife sexually. If he knows he can always resort to using his hands if something else should fail, he'll feel less pressure to perform in one specific way next time—and therefore probably do better as a result.

Think of it as an assignment—and not a bad one at that! Let your husband lead you to orgasm however he is capable of doing it, and don't be reserved with your words of encouragement about how he can always satisfy you. By doing this, you can turn a potentially humiliating and alienating experience into one that creates even more intimacy and fulfillment.

CHANGES FOR WOMEN

You women have a more dramatic marker of your aging process: it's called menopause. Psychologically, menopause marks a dramatic turning point in your sexuality. Suddenly sexuality is no longer connected with conceiving a child. Even if you have taken precautions for decades, there's still something different about sexual relations once conception becomes impossible. Now it's about intimacy and pleasure.

And there's nothing wrong with that.

There's no reason for menopause to dampen a woman's sex life. In many instances, women often feel more sexually invigorated. Yes, some women use menopause as an excuse to avoid what they've long found sexually or physically unfulfilling. But in most instances, there isn't a biological reason women should lose interest in sex during this period. Though women do experience a drop in estrogen, estrogen itself is not directly connected with sexual desire and response. Of course, the withdrawal of estrogen from a woman's body creates other symptoms that might put sexual thoughts on the back burner—hot flashes being the most well-known of them—but once a woman has passed through menopause, she may be freer than ever before to explore new sexual horizons. Even the drop in estrogen can now be regulated through estrogen patches.

The response to menopause is so individual that I dread

using any generalizations. Some women have told me they seemed to lose all desire for sexual intimacy, while another client intimated, a twinkle in her eye, "The day after the kids left the house Jim and I started using every room and every piece of furniture—and I mean *every.*"

Another major stepping-stone that often accompanies aging is a hysterectomy. Ladies, this is a major operation some of you take a little too casually. You get up too early, you drive too early, you start lifting too early, you have sex too early, and major consequences can follow. I know what I'm talking about: My wife, Sande, had one, and like many women, she felt guilty about taking so much time off. Plan on a good six to eight weeks to heal.

Husbands reading this book might be jumping off their chairs right now. "Six to eight weeks? Leman, are you crazy?"

Six weeks without intercourse doesn't necessarily mean six weeks without sexual expression and love. Couples can get creative at these junctures in life. To be sure, Mr. Happy rarely thinks, *I'll just take an eight-week vacation,* so a loving wife will do all she can to find creative ways to help relieve her husband's libido.

One of the great benefits for women who are older is that the greatest enemy of sex, weariness, may not be quite so strong. Most people have more time in their later years, and they often have fewer demands. You don't have to worry about whether a toddler is going to knock on your door and ask you for a drink of water. You don't have to play taxi driver all afternoon and come to bed exhausted. Your periods will stop, and since many couples prefer not to engage in sexual intimacy during a woman's period, as a couple you'll gain another five days a month of sexual availability.

Physically, you'll need to take extra care of your genitals. Once the estrogen levels drop, your vaginal walls will become thinner and dryer. You'll need to use lubrication, and your husband may, on occasion, need to take it easier, as a sharp thrust might cause pain instead of pleasure.

Incidentally, one of the best ways to maintain your sexual fitness into your sixties and seventies is to maintain your level of sexual activity. Masters and Johnson demonstrated that older women who engaged in sexual relations on at least a weekly basis lubricated more efficiently than women who abstained for long periods of time. The old adage, "use it or lose it" is quite accurate when it comes to sex.

I hope your attitude doesn't resemble that of Margaret, who came into my office with a decidedly unhappy husband. After just a few moments in the counseling room, Margaret's husband, Jerry, told me that Margaret had basically signed off any future sexual relations.

Margaret didn't deny this. She said, "Look, Dr. Leman, I really think I've served my time. I've never been all that much into sex, and frankly, Jerry hasn't been that creative. Even so, I've been faithful and dutiful for thirty-four years. Don't you think that's enough?"

We talked some about Jerry's lack of creativity, but when it came time to address Margaret, I answered her question, "Don't you think that's enough?" with a firm, "No, I don't."

In fact, I posed another question. "How would you feel if Jerry said, 'All right, Margaret, I've supported you with my paycheck for thirty-four years. Now that I'm going on a pension, I've decided I don't want to support you anymore. You're going to have to find your own place to live and your own source of income. I've done my time, and now I want to be a bit more selfish.'

"You see, Margaret," I continued, "marriage is for life—and the commitments we make are for life as well. The route you're taking is a very dangerous one. In fact, if your aim is to spiritually emasculate Jerry and turn him into an angry husband instead of a thankful husband, keep this up. You'll see the ugly head of selfishness rear itself faster than you can believe.

"When the apostle Paul says that the 'two shall become one,' he's expressing a commandment. That oneness includes physical oneness, expressed in sexual intimacy. Physical oneness enriches all aspects of oneness. You can't refuse one aspect and demand another.

"But just as importantly, you're making a unilateral decision that has dual consequences. Just because you're done with sex doesn't mean Jerry is, and what is he supposed to do now? Has he ever been unfaithful to you?"

"No."

"And this is how you reward him? Tell me, Margaret, why do otherwise seemingly respectable men—who by all other standards seem to be pretty good guys—end up shocking everybody by having an affair? Or get caught going to strip clubs on a business trip? Although becoming involved in affairs or pornography is never morally acceptable, and a man's actions shouldn't be based on his wife's behavior, it seems to me that a lot of this happens because basic needs aren't being met in their marriage. A sixty-year-old man wants to feel wanted and needed and prized just as much as a thirty-year-old man. That bride of his may look quite different thirty years down the road, but she's still his honey, the love of his life; and he still wants her to want him."

Margaret eventually understood that the solution wasn't to stop having sex, but to help Jerry be more sensitive in his lovemaking.

ARM IN ARM

You've probably seen them just as I have: a decidedly older couple walking arm in arm at the mall. One has difficulty walking, so she's being supported by her spouse. Maybe they stop to buy a cookie or an ice cream cone and have a huddle to decide just what it is they want. Then they invariably share their selections. The wife might wipe her husband's mouth just before she kisses it.

They are like two halves of one whole. Faithful to each other for four, five, or even six decades, they can't imagine life apart from each other. I'm sure they're not acting like gymnasts in the bedroom; no one is hanging from the chandelier; and the *Kama Sutra* has long since been put away or sold. But look at that man's face, and you see one happy boy. He still knows how to please his wife, and she still wants what he has.

Emotionally, there's nothing better than that. One-night stands don't come even close to the wondrous experience of making love to the same person one thousand times.

That older couple is a truly beautiful picture, a stunningly profound portrait of lifelong love that our Creator wants us to experience. Sex in the winter is a wonderful thing. It becomes near miraculous when it's preceded by sex in the spring, summer, and fall—all with the same person.

A Whale of a Tail

Take a look at my picture on the back cover of this book. Go ahead—I'll wait for you.

Have that picture in your mind? Good. What you didn't see was the 90 percent of me that's attached to my neck. You just saw my head, so I'll have to fill in a few details. I used to weigh less than I do now. That's a gentle way of saying you'd have to search a bit to find my abdomen—I certainly don't sport the "six pack" look found on the covers of men's health magazines. I gave up wearing certain kinds of pants and certain tailored shirts decades ago.

I was lucky, however, to marry a "looker." My wife's a knockout, as pretty as they come. See if you can believe this: Sande's dress size is nearly identical to what it was when we got married. Me, I'm like a whale. One of my greatest fears is that when I go to the beach, take off my shirt, and lie down in the white sand, a bunch of tree huggers will come out and try to push me back into the ocean.

Whenever men meet Sande and me for the first time, they spend the first five seconds giving my wife the big fish-eye look over, then they glance at me, utterly perplexed, as if I should have married a pit bull or something.

I may not be a candidate for an underwear ad, but I'll bet most of *you* wouldn't qualify for the cover of *Playboy* or *Playgirl*—even if you would be willing to pose (which, hopefully, you wouldn't).

You know what? Very few of us could.

Here's a helpful exercise: Sit down sometime on a bench in a mall and just look at the people for fifteen to twenty minutes. How many of them would you describe as gorgeous or handsome?

If your experience has been at all like mine, you'd answer, "Not very many." The vast majority of us fall somewhere slightly above, or slightly below, average. Does this mean the rest of us are married to people whose bodies don't excite us? Do we think only Hollywood leading men and women can have satisfying sex lives? I certainly don't.

I may not have an Olympic athlete's body, but boy, I love giving what I do have to my wife. Women in particular need to have the same attitude, but it's a little more difficult for them. A positive body image with women just doesn't come as easily—at least not to most of the women I've talked to. According to a *Psychology Today* survey, more than half of all American women dislike their overall appearance.[41] From my practice, I suspect it's *way* over half. Even women who know it's "politically correct" to accept their body type, still, in private, have a tendency to look in the mirror and wince. It's a fact that women are generally more self-conscious about their

[41]Cited in Nancy Stedman, "Love Your Body," *Redbook*, May 2001, 46.

bodies than men. Just compare the amount of time the average wife spends in front of a mirror, touching up her face, her makeup, her hair, and putting lotion on her skin, with the amount of time her husband does. If he isn't shaving, he's probably not paying too much attention to what he looks like. I don't know if I've *ever* put lotion on my skin, and the only time any makeup has touched my face is when someone put it there before I went on television.

I can't tell you how many times I've seen two women get together, and one of them says, "Oh, I just looove your haircut. It's soooo cute."

"Oh, don't even mention my hair," the other woman protests. She then pulls out a picture from a magazine—apparently, this is what her hair was *supposed* to look like, but the woman who cut it left it too long here and didn't layer it right there, and her face now looks too round, and she doesn't don't know what she's going to do for the big dinner party on Saturday night!

Compare that to when my buddy Moonhead and I get together: "Hey, Leman, you got a haircut, huh?"

"Yeah."

That's the entire conversation!

This obsession over how you look can lead to some pretty cruel habits. A lot of you women don't think of yourselves as cruel, but you really are. No, you'd never intentionally hurt someone else's feelings—but consider how cruel you can be *to yourself.*

Dr. Thomas Cash, author of *The Body Image Workbook,* asks an intriguing question: "Would you let someone else criticize you the way you criticize yourself?"[42]

Now why am I talking about this here? Your body image will greatly impact your ability to give yourself fully to your

---

[42]Stedman, "Love Your Body," 46.

spouse. You may not have the smile of Julia Roberts, the breasts of a *Sports Illustrated* swimsuit model, or legs that would fit into a pair of fashion designer jeans—but I can guarantee you one thing: Your husband doesn't want to wait until you lose ten or fifteen pounds before you have sex again!

IMPROVING YOUR BODY IMAGE

I realize I've said this many times already, but in case it hasn't gotten through yet, let me say it again: Wives, sight is an incredibly powerful turn-on for a man. You may think you don't measure up, and thus rob your husband of letting him look at you, but what you're doing is counterproductive.

Let's say a woman is small-breasted and therefore has a poor self-image. (By the way, I'm not agreeing with the axiom that small means inferior. That's a ridiculous assumption in my view, but it's a common one, so I'm giving in to popular misconceptions.) When this woman buys a woman's magazine and takes a look through the ads, she doesn't see anyone who resembles her. When she passes billboards on the way home from the store, she doesn't see giant photos of flat-chested women hawking beer or cigarettes. And when she turns on the television at night, the sitcom moms invariably wear tight sweaters with just a touch of cleavage showing.

When the woman gets undressed at night, she sees her own small breasts and her growing thighs and thinks to herself, *Why can't I take five pounds from there and put it here?*

The problem is, she assumes her husband won't be turned on by her body because she doesn't look like the women in the magazine. What she fails to remember is that her husband doesn't look like the men in the magazine! They're all myths, spray-painted and touched-up ideals that approximate a false sense of beauty.

Maybe your problem isn't being flat-chested. On the contrary, you've become a victim of gravity, and you feel like your husband would need to be a weight lifter to keep your breasts from falling down, should you remove your bra. Or perhaps you developed your own set of love handles five or ten years ago, and you're afraid that wearing lingerie would make your husband laugh instead of get turned on.

Maybe you've given birth to three kids and you've got the stretch marks to prove it. Perhaps you gained seventeen pounds after the last birth and still haven't lost it. You feel completely unlovely and when your husband says how attracted he is to you, you shun his advances and cover up.

He says your body turns him on, but you won't show it to him.

Don't get me wrong. I feel for you, because I know you're being bombarded with this perfect-body garbage all day long. But I want you to try to begin listening to the man who loves you rather than all the men who want to sell you something. Since sight is so important to your husband, you need to wrestle through to the point where you can feel good enough about yourself to use your beauty to entice your husband.

One husband told me he has been praying for years that his wife could see herself through his eyes. He delights in her beauty, and he even said that throughout the process of her bearing children and afterwards, there has never been a time when he hasn't found her physically appealing. But she still doesn't entirely believe it. That's sad.

Here are a few tips to help this process along.

1. Focus on your strengths.

Did you realize that even the *Sports Illustrated* swimsuit models have certain features that are emphasized and ones that get hidden? The photographer may focus on a woman's legs, rear end, back, or bosom—and the person in charge of that issue will have each model wear suits that emphasize her most appealing features, while the photographer will photograph her in poses that bring those features to the forefront.

Learn to present yourself to your spouse in the same way. Maybe you want to emphasize your eyes, your legs, or something else. Learn to accept that as your strength, and—at least in front of your spouse—shamelessly flaunt it to full effect.

If your breasts are your strong point, buy lingerie that brings all the attention to your chest. If your best-selling point is your eyes, or maybe your mouth, wear makeup that will draw your husband's attention to those features. Use what you have to full effect, and don't worry about the rest.

2. The equal time rule.

Do you ever catch yourself knocking down your physical looks with comments like these?

"Look at those thighs—they're just disgusting."

"Oh, I hate this stringy hair. I can't do a thing with it!"

"If my breasts fall any farther, I'll have to put shoes on them!"

If so, Dr. Cash offers the "equal time rule," which I heartily endorse: You need to give equal time to the positive parts of your body. It's only fair. You owe yourself one compliment for every criticism. Spend *at least* as much time thinking about your positive points as you do your negative ones.

Remember, you weren't put together on overtime at a factory in New Jersey. You were designed, crafted, molded, and sculpted by no less a designer than God himself. And when he birthed you, he sat back, smiled, and said, "This is good."

Yeah, you may not have taken the best care of what God gave you; you may have adopted a few habits that don't leave you looking your best. But don't insult your Creator by ignoring the wonderful qualities he placed in you. Learn to be *thankful*:

"Thank you, God, for these eyes."

"Lord, I'm so thankful for these hands. Help me to use them to love my husband and kids."

"Thank you, Lord, for giving me lips to kiss my husband."

"Thank you Lord, for giving me legs to wrap around my spouse, and breasts to entice his eyes."

3. Stay away from situations you know you can't handle.
If body image is a problem area for you, enlist support for situations where you know you're in trouble. If shopping for a swimsuit is guaranteed to get you down, ask a friend to come along and do your best to make it fun. Don't feel pressured into buying a swimsuit that makes you feel conspicuous. There's nothing wrong with putting shorts over the bottom of a suit to cover up a little bit more. Most suits today are way too immodest—and not very practical for anyone who is over eighteen or who plans to do more than lie on a blanket while she wears it.

Some of you should get rid of the scales in your house. Others of you need to reconsider where you keep mirrors. Craft an environment that doesn't work against you.

4. Learn to enjoy sensual moments.
I'm not talking about sex here. I'm talking about the feel of ice-cold tea on a hot summer day. I'm talking about being surrounded by hot water in a luxurious bath on a winter night, or better yet, sitting in a spa with a light snowfall. I'm talking about your husband's hands rubbing lotion into your feet. God has given us more nerve endings than we'll ever know or even use. Become more aware of them; revel in them; let your senses come alive.

As you become more sensually aware, you'll realize the depth of sex that goes beyond looking like Ken or Barbie. The body is a wonderful thing, and most of the body can't be seen. Unless you're a medical student or doctor, you've probably never seen one of those nerve endings that so deliciously come alive when they're touched in just the right place.

A man would rather go to bed with a sensually aware woman packing a few extra pounds than a perfectly manicured Barbie who is closed and frigid and warped by being so self-conscious.

5. Have sex more frequently.

Do you want to look younger? Are you afraid time has taken its toll on your sexual appeal? If so, I have a great and fun solution for you: Have lots of sex!

David Weeks, a neuropsychologist at Royal Edinburgh Hospital in Scotland suggests that, "More orgasms may lead to a greater release of hormones that bolster your immune system and slow premature aging."[43] This was in response to a ten-year study of more than 3,500 men and women. Those who looked the youngest reported far more active sex lives than the older-looking participants.

Psychologically, how we feel about ourselves greatly affects how we actually begin to look. When you engage in regular sexual relations, that very act affirms your body, because your husband is loving it, adoring it, and caressing it. When you feel sexy, you look sexier.

One husband told me that his wife was a "hottie." When I saw her, I almost had to laugh. She is not a conventional beauty. In fact, in many ways, you could even say that nature has not been kind to her.

But you'd never convince her husband of many years of that. Why? He intimated that she wears him out in bed. She can't get enough of him, and he can't get enough of her. The average man might look at her and see a homely face and an unbecoming body, but her husband sees a woman he has enjoyed, delighted in, tasted, touched, smelled, licked, caressed, ogled, and, in every way, adored. Frequent sex with a person can literally change how he or she looks at you.

HOW TO LOSE TEN POUNDS IMMEDIATELY

You want to lose ten pounds, immediately, the next time you jump into bed? Here's a psychologist's trick: smile. Look se-

[43]Pamela Lister and Janis Graham, "More Sex = Younger Looks!" *Redbook*, June 2001, 80.

ductive. Maybe even growl. When you're comfortable with your own body, your spouse will feel more comfortable with it, too. Your facial expressions and your attitude have a far bigger effect on your appearance than you could ever know. Use them to full effect.

Another way to shave off a little weight is to darken the room. Candlelight is sexy, with the added benefit of creating shadows that still let you hide a few flaws. If the softer appearance of a candle makes you feel better, buy them by the bunch!

Now, how do you *add* ten pounds? Become so self-conscious about a particular body part that you're always pointing it out and criticizing it. Come to bed making a big deal about covering up. Act like you're ashamed, embarrassed, and mortified.

Take it from a psychologist: People often get treated according to the image they have of themselves. Kids who get picked on at school often *expect* to get picked on. Boys with lots of confidence look more attractive. I believe that a positive or negative self-image is worth ten pounds either way.

AFFIRMING YOUR SPOUSE

A spouse makes all the difference when it comes to body comfort. Ladies, your man needs to know that you desire him, love handles and all. And men, your wives need to know that stretch marks and the inevitable effect of gravity haven't stopped your sexual interest. Here's how one woman described the way her husband's acceptance changed her view of herself:

"I hated my body. Whenever I looked into a mirror, I saw only my small breasts and my large thighs. I was embarrassed to change my clothes in front of anyone. Then, when I married, sex was always tense for me because I was afraid to be seen from certain angles. But Craig changed all that. He smiled as I undressed. He told me how lovely my body was.

He touched me in ways that made me believe that he really meant it. Then I was okay and I could finally relax enough to enjoy sex. Since that time I've learned to even show off a little. And now I'm not afraid to initiate sex myself."[44]

Do you get it, guys? Sometimes you are going to have to work hard to convince your wife that you find her physically attractive. She's receiving false messages and being bombarded by idealistic, airbrushed images virtually every time she goes to the store or opens up a magazine; you need to let her know you find her very sexy and attractive. More often than not, you'll benefit from this every bit as much as she does. Women need adoring words from their husbands—but not just when the husband wants sex. Just as you're leaving the house, or walking into church—a place where your wife knows you can't have any ulterior motives—pause, take in an eyeful, and tell her, "Honey, you look absolutely fantastic. I'm so proud to be seen with you today."

We live in a world that glorifies youth, uncommitted sex, and bodies that require a ridiculous amount of self-serving time in the gym. Let's turn that around. Let's reaffirm the bodies of women who have generously and selflessly produced life for one, two, three, or four babies. Let's appreciate those men who work hard to support their families and who don't have time to stop off at the gym and lift weights because they're eager to get home and play with their kids.

The best way to do this is to enjoy your spouse's body to the fullest. Explore it. Revel in it. Play with it. Touch it. Praise it.

Your body is a wonderful thing. It's one of the best gifts you can ever give to your spouse. Don't be selfish. Be generous, and enjoy the results!

[44]Sanna with Miller, *How to Romance*, 89.

A Very Good Gift, Indeed

One night I treated Sande to the dinner of a lifetime. We went to a restaurant called the Oak Room at the Drake Hotel, right off Michigan Avenue in downtown Chicago.

Sande loved it; she has Martha Stewart–type tastes, and I got a real chuckle out of her summary: "Delicious, beautiful food at that buffet, and no Jell-O in sight." Most cafeterias, cafes, and buffets always greet you with colorful Jell-O and gaudy pies—but not the Oak Room.

Of course, if you're into Jell-O, I could suggest some other places to go—Sande and I have been there and done that, too. There's a place in our life for buffets with Jell-O, but some nights, we really enjoy going upscale.

You're already tracking with me, I'm sure. I want to close by telling you what I told several of the couples I interviewed while writing this book. My prayer for you (yes, prayer) is that you will fully experience all the joys, delights, and pleasures your Creator has designed for you to know in sexual intimacy. I want you to take your sex life to new heights, to literally pray that God would help both of you to experience sexual intimacy like you never have before.

Why do I want this? Because if you pray about growing sexual intimacy and then experience it, your marriage will become stronger than it has ever been. You'll be better parents, you'll be more faithful believers, more productive community members—yes, even better people.

Good, healthy sex is a marvelous invention that does wonderful things for us physically, relationally, psychologically, and even spiritually. People who have been scarred by unholy sex or who are drowning in a sexual addiction may have a difficult time experiencing just how energizing good, holy sex can be. To them, sex is a burden instead of a blessing. But if you can turn that corner into holy sex, you'll discover an avenue of pure passion and delight that'll make Disneyland look like Siberia in the dead of winter.

One of the wonderful things about married sexual intimacy is that it is a lifelong journey. Where you are now doesn't need to limit where you will be five years from now. Your relationship will evolve, as I have watched thousands of couples evolve.

Sometimes this evolution is shocking to one or both spouses.

I can think of one woman in particular, who's very conservative. She wouldn't think of parking in any space where there weren't two clearly delineated lines—and if she's driving the family minivan, she won't even park in one of those spaces marked "compact."

But when her husband gets her in bed, she experiences a freedom, a joy, and a passion that would rouse half the neighborhood if it weren't for the insulation on the outside walls. Not all the time, mind you, but enough so her husband recognizes he is a very blessed man.

Sometimes a married sexual feast will be a real gourmet experience. At other times it will resemble fast food. Sometimes a couple might focus on "dessert." Other times a couple might want a full meal. The best thing is, it's all good! God is great—and in sex, he has given us a very wondrous gift. I pray you will enjoy it more and more.

Here's my final assignment, my parting words. Pray this prayer right now: "Dear God, help me to know what to do to please my mate sexually tonight—and then give me the desire to do it."

If you pray this prayer with sincerity, it can change your marriage. Why don't you try it and see?

OTHER RESOURCES BY
DR. KEVIN LEMAN

Books
Adolescence Isn't Terminal
The Real You: Become the Person You Were Meant to Be
Say Good-Bye to Stress
The Birth Order Connection
What a Difference a Daddy Makes
Making Children Mind without Losing Yours
Making Sense of the Men in Your Life
Becoming a Couple of Promise
Becoming the Parent God Wants You to Be (with Dave and
   Neta Jackson)
The New Birth Order Book
Women Who Try Too Hard
When Your Best Is Not Good Enough
Bringing Up Kids without Tearing Them Down
Living in a Step-Family without Getting Stepped On
Unlocking the Secrets of Your Childhood Memories (with
   Randy Carlson)
Sex Begins in the Kitchen

Video Series
Making Children Mind without Losing Yours—parenting edition
Making Children Mind without Losing Yours—public school
   edition for teachers, in-service sessions, PTA events
Bringing Peace and Harmony to the Blended Family
*Single Parenting that WORKS! Raising Well-Balanced Children
   in an Off-Balance World*
Making the Most of Marriage

ABOUT DR. KEVIN LEMAN . . .
PRACTICAL WISDOM
WITH A SMILE

An internationally known psychologist, award-winning author, radio and television personality, and speaker, Dr. Kevin Leman has taught and entertained audiences worldwide with his wit and commonsense psychology.

The best-selling "relationship doctor" has made house calls for numerous radio and television programs, including *The View* with Barbara Walters, *Today, Oprah,* CBS's *The Early Show, Live with Regis and Kelly, Focus on the Family* with Dr. James Dobson, and *LIFE Today* with James Robison. Dr. Leman is a frequent contributor to CNN's *American Morning* and has served as a contributing family psychologist to *Good Morning America.*

Dr. Leman is also the founder and president of Couples of Promise, an organization designed and committed to helping couples remain happily married.

Some of Dr. Leman's best-selling titles include:

- *The New Birth Order Book*
- *Making Children Mind without Losing Yours*
- *Bringing Up Kids without Tearing Them Down*
- *Sex Begins in the Kitchen*
- *Making Sense of the Men in Your Life*
- *The Birth Order Connection*
- *When Your Best Is Not Good Enough*
- *Adolescence Isn't Terminal: It Just Feels Like It*
- *Becoming a Couple of Promise*
- *What a Difference a Daddy Makes*

- *Sheet Music: Uncovering the Secrets of Sexual Intimacy in Marriage*
- *Say Good-Bye to Stress*
- *The Real You: Become the Person You Were Meant to Be*
- *Keeping Your Family Strong in a World Gone Wrong*

Dr. Leman's professional affiliations include the American Psychological Association, American Federation of Radio and Television Artists, National Register of Health Services Providers in Psychology, and the North American Society of Adlerian Psychology.

Dr. Leman attended North Park College. He received his bachelor's degree in psychology from the University of Arizona, where he later earned his master's and doctorate degrees. Originally from Williamsville, New York, he and his wife, Sande, live in Tucson. They have five children.

For speaking-engagement information for businesses, churches, and civic organizations, please contact:

Dr. Kevin Leman
P.O. Box 35370
Tucson, Arizona 85740
Phone: (520) 797-3830
Fax: (520) 797-3809
Web site: www.realfamilies.com